The Millennium Myth

The Ever-Ending Story

by Sean M. O'Shea and Meryl A. Walker

The Millennium Myth

The Ever-Ending Story

by Sean M. O'Shea and Meryl A. Walker

Humanics Trade
P.O.Box 7400
Atlanta, GA 30357

The Millennium Myth

A Humanics Publication

Published simultaneously in the United States and Canada.

Humanics Trade Publications are an imprint of and published by Humanics
Limited, a division of Humanics Publishing Group, Inc.
Its trademark, consisting of the words "Humanics Trade" and
the portrayal of a Pegasus, is Registered in U.S. Patent and
Trademark Office and in other countries.

Humanics Limited, P.O. Box 7400, Atlanta, GA 30357

Printed in the United States of America

ISBN: 0-89334-273-4

Editing and Book Design
by Nancy Brand, Laura Ross, and Christopher Walker
Cover Design by Jill Dible and Laura Ross

— ACKNOWLEDGEMENTS —

We would like to acknowledge Ryan and Erin,
because we love them,
and Nancy Brand, our editor, for her grace,
patience, and encouragement.

ABOUT THE AUTHORS

Sean M. O'Shea has been an educator for more than twenty years. He holds a doctorate in Education Administration from Teacher's College, Columbia University. He has served as an adjunct professor in the graduate programs of Fordham University and St. John's University. He has two children, and lives in Manhattan with his wife, the co-author of this book.

Meryl A. Walker is a teacher/counselor with more than twenty years of experience in education. She holds one master's degree in Special Education, another in Psychological Counseling, and a certificate in Alcohol and Substance Abuse Counseling. She is presently working with acutely and chronically ill children and their families. In addition she counsels teens and adults with substance abuse problems. She lives in Manhattan with her husband, the co-author of this book.

TABLE OF CONTENTS

CHAPTER FOUR
Eschatology and Historical Events

CHAPTER FIVE
The Millennium in America

Sean M. O'Shea and Meryl A. Walker

The Last Judgment (above), and *Angels of the Lord Smiting the Enemies of the Israeltes* (Below), from the *Ulrecht Psalter,* Illumination, c. 820-32 A.D.

Chapter One

The End:
From the Beginning

"The first angel sounded, and there followed hail and fire mingled with blood, and they were cast upon the earth: and the third part of the world was burnt up, and all green grass was burnt up... and as it were a great mountain burning with fire was cast into the sea: and the third part of the sea became blood; and a third part of the creatures who were in the sea, and had life, died; and the third part of the ships were destroyed... And there fell a great star from heaven, burning as it were a lamp, and it fell upon a third part of the rivers, and upon the fountains of waters and many men died of the waters because they were made bitter... and the third part of the sun was smitten, and the third part of the moon, and the third part of the stars; so as the third part of them was darkened, and the day shone not for the third part of it, and the night likewise. And I beheld, and heard an angel flying through the midst of heaven, saying with a loud voice:

Woe, woe, woe, to the inhabitants of earth..."
Revelations, Chapter 8:4-13

The End of the World... is there a more powerful nightmare? The brief excerpt presented above is part of the Book of Revelations, the last book of the Christian bible. In contrast to the first book, *Genesis*, a book of Creation and the promise of beginnings, *Revelations* is a terrible vision of the final days of mankind. John of Patmos, or St. John the Divine, was a disciple of Jesus Christ, and wrote this "revelation", or dramatic disclosure, while in exile on the island of Patmos (Greece) during the first century. It is said that this scenario of the future demise of mankind was reported to John by an angel in a dream.

For the following nineteen hundred years, the contents of this angel's treatise occupied at least a corner of the consciousness of Christians throughout the world. Its awesome, as well as gory, imagery has inspired millions over the last two millennia. At its best,

Revelations was an inspiration, often a motivator, to lead a life fit to be judged. At its worst, Revelations became an excuse to murder and butcher in the name of the Christian God, as in the Crusades and countless other acts of violence and war committed in the hope of currying the favor of a God left mute in the perversive interpretation of Divine Word.

While the Christian perspective on the end of the world is the most common in the Western Hemisphere, it is by no means the only view. Other cultures have their own interpretations of the end of the world, which we will examine in the course of this book. Regardless of orientation, the change of a century, as well as a millennium, is upon us, and with these events come prophecies and conceptions that imply both destruction and/or a transformation to a new and better age. This event is referred to as the *Millennium.* The cultural tradition around this event is referred to as *myth.*

The Millennium Myth is the story of the end of the world. Millennium literally refers to a period of one thousand years. Figuratively, however, the word describes the end of the world as we know it, the end of our current age. For some, the Millennium is the long anticipated thousand-year period in which evil is enchained and the world lives in the glow of holiness. To others, the Millennium connotes the predicted day of reckoning; the time of the destruction of the world. And still others feel that the Millennium is a transformational event, an evolutionary step, in which this existence will be replaced by a Golden Age. All interpretations and perspectives, save one, indicate that the Millennium is a pivotal, if not final, historical event. Those who dismiss its importance are dissenters who say that the Millennium is fiction.

Myth defies a single definition or description. A contemporary, critical view of myth may equate it with fabrication.[1] Indeed, when traced back to its Greek origins, myth translates as "tale," or "story," with no connection to truth.[2] However, to dismiss myth on those grounds is to overlook the truths that are at its foundations. Myth is inherently connected to the environment of its origin. It reflects the thought patterns by which a culture distinguishes itself, knows itself, and develops its own unique set of values, norms, and mores. Mankind has lived by myth, died in the comfort of its promise, and even committed murder in its name.[3] For many cultures, myth is the constant that views past, present, and future not as different times, but as *timeless.* Myth, then, is the thread that holds eras together.[4] The impact of myth is so powerful that it may be part of the structure of our unconsciousness, even genetically encoded.[5]

The Millennium Myth is an ever-ending story because it is an inveterate enigma; although perpetually present, it is yet unfinished. We find its roots in our distant past, in the antiquity peopled by our shared ancestors. It is part of an ongoing epoch, which found our predecessors looking towards the future with the heady mix of fear and anticipation we still feel today. But how long might that future last? Will it end tomorrow, or with the mathematical turn of years: 1000, 2000, 2001? Perhaps the Millennium will be the outcome of a significant event. Will a coronation, a war, or a revolution be the precipitating occurrence? Or will it be a heavenly phenomenon, such as the arrival of a comet or the vision of a supernova?

The Millennium scenario is such an omnipresent part of world cultural lore that it can be assigned as an "enigmatic, inherited image"; a part of the "phenomenon of self induced belief"[6] so intense in our minds that it is transmitted for cultural and collective retention. Perhaps we have been *programmed* to expect a Millennium, and the intensity and efficiency of that programming will be measured by the millions of people who are anticipating the upcoming millennium with dire earnestness. The suicides connected to the appearance of the Hale-Bopp comet are only a sampling of the extreme drama produced by Millennial fervor.

THE ORIGIN OF MYTH

The birth of myth is found in antiquity, and the existence of myth can be tied to a genuine need. The world presented numerous dilemmas to our ancestors. However, as the fundamental needs of food, shelter, and clothing were met and communities grew, the rudiments of societies sprouted and questions abounded. Natural phenomena confounded observers. Thunder, rain, and budding seeds were miraculous events. The passage of time, the movements of the sun, the appearance and disappearance of the moon, and the shimmering stars engendered queries. Was the rising of the sun a certainty? What were our origins? Why are we here? What is the ultimate destiny of our existence? Myths would respond to questions such as these, and would thus serve as a precursor to religion and science.[7]

In contemporary culture, we have a voracious appetite for detective prose written about fictitious heroes, such as Sherlock Holmes and Miss Marple; these characters share the uncanny gift of solving mysteries, as well as a knack for making the seemingly inexplicable plainly evident. In addition, we open an amused, cynical, but curious ear to the predictions of psychics, seers, and prophets, from Nostradamus to Jean Dixon.

Ancient cultures also craved definitive answers to the mysteries of both the origin and termination of their existence. The questions asked by our forebears surely included the enduring questions posed in every era: "Where did this world come from?"; "When will this world end?"; and "What happens after the end of this world?" From each of the many and varied world cultures, there emerged someone who *would* answer these questions, who charismatically and emphatically stated the solutions to the riddles of the universal mysteries. These extraordinary people, in addition to seeing themselves as unfailingly correct, shared one other distinct characteristic: they had endured a metamorphic experience called *rapture,*[8] the feeling of being carried away from this world into an otherworldly state of being.

RAPTURE

As long-traveled voyagers in the journey of life, we can all relate to the first of the four noble truths of the Buddha: 'life is suffering'. We have all suffered, many of us more than we would have chosen. But we have also known unfortunate persons who have suffered far more than we have, far more than seems imaginable. A very select few have actually been *transformed* by their suffering, demonstrating that strife may eventually benefit the sufferer.[9] In Judaic tradition, Moses was transformed, as were his people, by forty years of extreme hardship in the desert. Christian tradition depicts Jesus' transformation as occurring after he encountered challenging visions and temptations during forty days in the desert. Buddha, under the bodhi tree, traversed the parameters of horror and seduction in human experience. Extended fasting, prolonged pain, extreme deprivation, traumatic crisis, or intensive meditation or prayer contribute to one's crossing the threshold into transcendent experience. An account of the practices of an Eskimo shaman[10] records that he consumed a single meal of water and meat over a period of *twenty-five days.* The account also reports that extreme fasting was felt by the shamans to be "the best way to attain knowledge of hidden things." This knowledge or state of being is experienced as a heightened state of awareness, understanding, and wisdom. This state of rapture is a primary credential on the transcendent vitae of seers, prophets, wizards, and sages throughout history.[11]

Rapture is not an unfamiliar concept to many of us. Our familiarity with rapture may come from our religious upbringing, or our readings about other traditions. It is not an experience confined to the leaders of a few prominent organized religions. Rapture has appeared in all cultures throughout history.

Having endured this rapture, the individual (seer) was driven to share the visions and impart the resultant wisdom to the members of the tribe, clan, or community. This was a task not so easily accomplished. How can one describe the indescribable? We all can recall times when we have awakened with the images of a dream still strikingly vivid, yet our words fail to accurately depict what we have experienced. The problem we share with the seers in this circumstance is the translation of extremely complex images from one medium (dreams, visions, hallucinations) into another medium that is comparatively rudimentary (words). The seer was faced with the task of explaining the awesome quality of his rapture in understandable terms, while at the same time impressing his listeners, and perhaps even frightening them, with his new sense of power.[12] Returning to the account of the Eskimo shamans, the villagers heard the revelations of ten deaths and resurrections by one shaman, and witnessed a woman's restoration of life by their local shaman.[13] Armed with such visions and experiences, as well as new-found wisdom, the seer would proceed to share his solutions to the mysteries of existence. The mysteries and secrets were unraveled in scenarios, stories, or tales, in what we now know as myth.

The important mysteries of existence that myths answer require an appropriate stage and suitable decorative props for their resolution. The stages upon which myths are set consist of nothing less formidable than the earth, the heavens, and the underworld. The props are nature itself, including the sun, the moon, and the stars. The actors are gods, giants, demons, and angels, as well as animals both real and imagined. The activities in the scenarios need to be worthy of the other elements. When myths were born, there was much respect for the power of magic. Knowing this, the authors of myth bestowed powers upon their characters that were not only impossible, but scarcely imaginable.[14] Perhaps the brief recounting of a creation myth from Zaire will illustrate this.

Mbombo is the creator-god. At the time of the beginning of all things, Mbombo exists in total darkness, in the waters that are the source of life. A terrible stomachache results in the sun, moon, and stars emerging from his belly. The passing of days has the new sun emitting light and evaporating the waters, producing dry land. Another stomachache produces the plants and animals of the earth. Finally, Mbombo produces people and the tools necessary for life.[15] In terms such as these, ancient cultures came to an understanding of the mysteries that had previously defied their attempts at comprehension. With remarkable similarities throughout cultures, myths dealt with the previously unknowable; the magic of creation, the gift of life, the fear of death, and the desperate hope that *something* followed death.

Mythology often explores how the natural occurrences on earth, such as day and night or the changing of the seasons, generated myth in order to be understood, forging attitudes that survive to this day.[16] Even in our self-perceived sophisticated culture, our sources of entertainment (television, books, or movies) still create a dramatic effect simply by using the setting of night or day. How many movies have begun their stories with a sunrise, or an alarm clock announcing that the sun has risen? Isn't a character walking, riding, or driving into the sunset a cliche for the end of a story or a film? Our sense of, and reaction to, these ongoing phenomena are as old as our awareness. With the rising of the sun, the promise of a day beginning reminds us of the gift of creation, of a world started anew, and of all possible potentials to be realized. In the light of day, the miracle of life thrives.

In contrast, the setting of the sun and the end of the day have very different associations. The end of the day provides a reminder that all things end, including ourselves and our world. As dawn is the harbinger of commencement, sunset is the precursor of termination. In the darkness of night that follows, we find the most productive medium for fear ever known. Through the ages, the night has been the premier forum for the release of the part of our humanity that we proactively hide from the light of day: our *dark* side, our shadow. We save our deepest anxieties, our strongest desires, our darkest ambitions, for the night. We safely achieve this dark side of our existence during our *dreams.*

THE DARK SIDE

It has been stated that "men were dreaming even when they were little more than apes."[17] Dreams are presented on the landscape where heart, mind, body, and spirit meet. On this landscape all the wonders of the universe can be witnessed, all impossibilities that can be imagined are, and all sensations are magnified as they are experienced. Visions that have provided the gift of human creativity, and even driven the establishment of religious movements, were born in dreams. But in the same way that day concedes to night, dreams of the glorious must sometimes give way to the terror of nightmares. And in these darkest of dreams, unspeakable horrors are committed, as we are voyeurs or even participants in circumstances that seem both otherworldly and our worldly at the same time. What is perhaps the best known nightmare in western civilization is that of John of Patmos, briefly excerpted at the beginning of this chapter. This dream is the basis of *Revelations.* In years beyond counting, on nights not easily forgotten, the awesome power of dreams has been unleashed. Among the endless reservoir of disturbing images are those of a world destroyed and humanity eliminated, whether via the wrath of a god, the retaliation of nature, an invasion from space, or the self-destruction of man.

In the many cycles that our ancestors witnessed and experienced (day and night, the crop cycle, the four seasons, or life and death), they were far too astute to miss the corresponding application to their entire world: *someday it too will end.* Besides the scenarios created by the seer in order to solve the mysteries of existence, there were also the stories that acknowledged an end to existence.

As an example, Teutonic-Norse tradition has created one of the most celebrated symbols of myth: *Yggdrasil,* the cosmic tree. The branches of this tree were of such size that its branches reached all possible worlds, and its roots reached both heaven and hell. This tree's import in its culture was formidable.[18] This mighty symbol of life fades in the 'end of days' scenario of the Teutonic-Norse culture. The consumption of its leaves and the gnawing of its roots by predators and serpents leave this once universal ash sick, its trunk decaying. This vision of ultimate calamity, catastrophe, and cataclysm was troubling and disturbing to the culture it sprang from. What made it more acceptable, without the culture experiencing total despair, was the recognition that even at a scale as large as the universe, a cycle would be concluded, and a new one would follow. In India, as another example, the universe appears to infinitely regenerate itself. An endless cycle of Creation-Destruction- New Creation scenarios take place over periods of years that approach infinity.[19]

MYTHOLOGY/ RELIGION

In the origins of myth, we have seen the efforts of humans to understand the mysteries of existence. To the select few with the experience of rapture, these unexplainable, "ineffable mysteries"[20] became clear through the illustration of myth. Myths were created so that individuals, and then entire cultures, could access the wisdom gleaned from the rapture achieved by others, and use that wisdom as guiding principles in their lives. Myth consists of using others' rapture wisdom for guidance; attempting to attain that rapture for oneself marks the transition to religion.

Most religions acknowledge the pain of our existence, as the Buddha did. What religions purport to offer is the methodology by which we can generate the transcendent state of rapture from pain. The transformation of the extreme distaste of pain into the ecstatic state of rapture seems to be clearly paradoxical. Paradox, it seems, is common in religion.[21] Some other notable paradoxes include "the last shall be first", "know that you are ignorant"[22], and "the sweetest songs tell the saddest thought."[23] Perhaps the most paradoxical, yet the most comforting is: "in death there is a new life."

Religion offers many benefits to its faithful. Perhaps the most notable benefit is the gift of promise. Life is a challenging exercise, regardless of era. The challenges simply change, whether by type or by intensity. Throughout the ages, religion has offered the comforting promise that existence, no matter how difficult or demeaning, is simply a prelude. For those who endured this existence with all the grace available to them, a life following the present one was promised. In this next life, the afterlife, their new existence would be characterized by glory.

The notion of death followed by life was not unfounded in the experience of our ancient ancestors. As attentive witnesses to their natural environment as the source of their survival, cultures were keenly aware of the analogies of life and the seasons. The onset of winter produced natural symptoms consistent with death: wrinkled and lifeless foliage rotted on the landscape while animals disappeared into hibernation, seeming to withdraw from existence. The world became silent, covered in a shroud of snow and ice. Nature itself seemed to be going through its own suffering, a victim of the potent and seemingly lethal grip of winter, strangling the very life of earth.

The months that followed, however, produced a miracle of the highest order: spring. What once appeared dead was now alive and renewed: the suffering of winter became the rapture of spring. Brown fields became carpets of green, as the death shroud of snow and ice disappeared as if by command from the warming sun. Flowers exploded into blossoms, leaves burgeoned from trees, animals cavorted across the earth once more. The power of these images convincingly persuaded our forebears that there *was* a life after death, and renewal after destruction.

To those purveyors of religion, the seers with visions, there was another message as well. The renewal of life in nature was the product of a sequence, an order, a ritual of events. Wouldn't the following of ritual provide the members of the clan or culture with a similar promise? What these rituals comprised for a particular culture was part, of course, of the seer's wisdom. In general, it was determined that *all* things had a beginning and an end. In our existence, there are day and night, winter and spring, birth and death, and creation and destruction. As *Ecclesiastes* says, "there is a time for all things under the heavens."

CYCLES

In parameters that have already been presented, nature seems to move in cyclical patterns. A cycle is simply a period in which events occur in the same sequence. That period can be as short as a day or as lengthy as a Mayan cycle which, as we will discuss later, lasts many thousands of years. What many cultures have developed over their own history is a calender. Each calendar was reflective of the culture's marking of time relative to its needs: the scheduling of time was related to their lifestyle. The perspective of time of an agricultural people would be different from that of a hunting people, and a culture that survived on trade would have still another time schedule. However, regardless of the economic orientation of the culture, all cultures organized their lives around a calendar that is consistent with our perception of a year: a complete seasonal cycle.[24] Certainly the year of antiquity for all cultures was not twelve months, three hundred sixty-five days. There were a variety of lengths to weeks, months, and the year.

What is important and remains constant throughout most cultures, regardless of the length of a year for any given society, is that this period of a year had a definite beginning and a definite end, events that were highlighted by ritual. And following that end, a new period would begin, as a new year.[25] This "periodic regeneration"[26] is a very significant illustration of early-millennial thought. The periodic regeneration of time suggests the recreation of the world, Creation revisited, as well as dictating the end of the present world. So in many ancient cultures, the end of the year translates as the end of time, as a Millennium. During that ending period, a number of rituals were conducted that confirmed the transitional time was at hand; an end and a beginning.

THE NEW YEAR

The New Year, the symbolic recreation of the world, implied the return to the innocence and purity of the first moments of time.[27] At the instant of creation, the world was free of evil, demons, sin, sickness, and disease. Rituals were conducted to aid in the purification of the culture. Demons were driven out by loud noises and cries, often being literally chased from the village by members of the community. Fasting and cleansing rites were also practiced, which purged the body, and by connection the spirit, of impurities. Animals or humans representatively bearing the transgressions and sins of the entire community were thrust from the village.[28] The commissions and omissions of the past year, as well as the implicative existence of that year's world, were efficiently eliminated.

In the creation of the world, ancient cultures recognized that the forces of the cosmos had to be brought into order. The mythology of most cultures agrees that prior to creation, there was chaos.[29] In the annual re-making of the world, then, the rituals would have to reflect the primordial chaos that existed before the original creation. Each culture had its creation myth, which included the condition of the cosmos prior to the intervention of the local deity. The scenario usually described in great detail, and on the grandest scale, the cosmological forces and personalities that struggled to bring harmony to formlessness. In some cultures, this struggle was re-enacted; presented to the culture by actors, as a reminder of their origins.[30] In Babylon, as illustrated by prominent scholars,[31] the revisiting of primordial chaos was maximally experienced. Societal constructs were eliminated, slaves became masters, rules were abolished, and orgies proliferated. The chaos awaiting creation was extant again. Did you ever wonder about the origin of all the commotion at Times Square every December 31?

RESURRECTION

Another attribute of the transition to the New Year was the resurrection of the dead. In some cultures, on the occasion of the renewal of time, the souls of the dead are said to rise and return to their villages, where they are well received and honored.[32] This seeming impossibility is actualized, because in the transition from the present year to the new year, chaos reigns, and time is non-existent. In the absence of time, the dead and the living are contemporaries.

The promise of a resurrection is a powerful motivator indeed. Death, that most feared of experiences, lost some of its sting. The seduction of resurrection, of course, did not come without a demand for an exacting commitment in exchange. Resurrection was a benefit provided to a very select group, namely those who followed the vision of a particular shaman, myth, or religion.

The image of another, new life was a powerful instrument for controlling the lives of large numbers of people. We will review several historical examples of this in later chapters, but for now, an excellent example is Pope Urban II calling the First Crusade. Eternal life was promised to those who died battling the evil hordes dwelling in the Holy Land. As a result, thousands assembled to fight this "Holy War", a war believed to be the precursor to The Last Judgement, the Millennium.

The components are now in place. A culture produces a seer, a shaman, who has had a transcendent experience because of an extreme hardship. The power of this leader grows as he recounts his experience in impressive yet understandable terms. Hard questions about existence now have answers as seen by the shaman. Among the mysteries answered are those that address the end of existence.

This is depicted as either a final or cyclical event, with the end of one existence transitioning into another for those select few who are the purified, the followers of the vision, and the recipients of the ultimate promise of a new life. We will see this scenario played over and over again; the ever-ending story of the Millennium Myth.

The depth of adherence to belief in the Millennium is hard to overstate. For your consideration, did you know that in the United States alone...

40% of the American public believes the Bible is the *literal* word of God?

80% believe they will appear before God on Judgement Day?

80% believe God works miracles?

50% believe in angels?[33]

Clearly, just in the United States, there are many *millions* of Christians whose religious tradition is tied to the vision of the word of the bible, including its Millennium presentation. The Millennium Myth is not an esoteric belief belonging to an austere group of people. Whether through religious orientation, training, or choice, this myth has a stronghold, or at least a vestige of influence, on nearly all of us. The Millennium Myth is, as all myths are, "an eternal mirror in which we see our selves".[34]

MILLENNIUM TERMINOLOGY

As you read through this book, there are words and terms that will appear that are pertinent to any exploration of the subject of this book. Some, such as *myth* and *rapture,* have already been presented. The following terms, some of which will be more familiar than others, are relevant to the Millennium and will appear repeatedly in this text as well as in other literature.

Anti-Christ is a formidable figure who is in absolute opposition to Christ, or one who appears as a false Christ. In the *Book of Revelations,* Anti-Christ is an ultimate evil force. He has the capacity to perform impressively, and easily collect followers. Over the course of Christian history, the badge of Anti-Christ has been cast on many figures perceived to be supremely evil: Nero, Caligula, Napoleon, Hitler, and most currently, Hussein. A number of popes have also worn this label during periods of political and doctrinal turmoil, such as during the Protestant Reformation, when Martin

The Apocalypse, Plate 1, Albrecht Dürer, 1498.

Luther was similarly denigrated.[35, 36]

Apocalypse usually refers to the *Book of Revelations,* the last book of the Christian bible, which depicts the suffering and turmoil of the last days of the human race. In its Greek origin, Apocalypse translates into *Revelation*, which means a revealing.[37] Generically, it can mean any writing that describes the final days, or any depiction of an ultimate struggle between good and evil, that is enacted on a cosmic landscape of extraordinary events.

Apocrypha are certain books without verifiable authors or authenticated text. These are books omitted from the Hebrew Bible, which are presented as a non-doctrinal attachment to the Protestant Bible, and are mostly included in the Catholic Bible. For our purposes, their value relates to other visions of the end of days.

Armageddon is the battlefield depicted in the *Book of Revelations.* It is the scene of the final battle between the forces of good and the powers of evil. The term is said to be derived from the Hebrew term *Har,* meaning mountain, and *Megiddo,* the location of a multitude of bloody battles.

Chiliasm is, very simply, the belief in the coming of the millennium. More analytically, the word is rooted in terminology that means "a thousand." In ancient documents, the term "chiliad" refers to the time cited in the Book of Revelations 20:3 where Satan is confined for one thousand years. This principle is not confined to Christian tradition. It has been interpreted, over many cultures, as a period when evil is destroyed by the powers of good.[38]

Eschatology translates as "discourse about the last things,"[39] and pertains to the final events of the existence of the present world, and to the life that is purported to follow. It includes the Second Coming, the Last Judgement, and the conclusion of history. Anticipation of a life after the present one may be a concept that is 200,000 years old.[40]

The Great Year is the duration of time required for the planets to return to the place they held at creation. Since this alignment occurred relative to the most significant event in history ≠ creation≠ its reoccurrence, according to this logic, would be concurrent with an equally monumental event. This event is thought to be the conclusion of the current world age.[41] The location of the planets at creation, obviously, can only be theorized. The length of *The Great Year*, which is the length of time from creation to the end of the world/current age, varies according to the seer. Estimates range from only 2,484 years to over 96 *million* years.[42] But how, you may ask, can we calculate the date of creation? Over the course of history, many people have tried, using clues from the bible, feeling that the date of creation could be calculated *exactly.* These interesting calculations will be explored later. One particularly notable calculation is that of Nostradamus, who is revered by many as the foremost prophet of all time.[43]

Millennium generically refers to the end of the current age. Implied in this concept is a transition from one age to the next that is marked by events of the most horrible nature: an apocaplyse. The thousand years that dictate this term refer to the period of the post-apocaplyse, when the forces of goodness and holiness will be triumphant. There is substantial disagreement over how the Book of Revelations is to be interpreted, and therefore, where the Millennium fits in the sequence of post-apocaplytic events.

- *Amillennarians* do not believe in a future one thousand-year reign of Christ. This view holds that the current age will end with the sudden manifestation of Christ, the resurrection of the redeemed, the consignment of the damned to Hell, and the end of the universe. This is the purported stance of the Catholic Church, as well as some Protestant denominations. This view originates with St. Augustine in 400 C.E.[44]

- *Premillennarians* adhere to the belief that the millennium in which Christ triumphantly reigns over earth will precede the The Last Judgement.

- *Postmillennarians* believe that the millennium represents a period in which spiritual restoration will prepare for the coming of Christ.

Parousia is a Greek term that is often used to indicate the Second Coming. It comes from the Greek word meaning "to be near."

Prophecy is a gift that has been bestowed on members of all cultures throughout history. Prophecy occurs when a vehicle, a prophet, transmits information received from some higher or otherworldly source. The purpose of the transmission is usually guidance, a warning against undesirable circumstances, or a vision of some future event. Among the circumstances that make prophecy problematic is the fact that the transmission of information often occurs in visions or dreams which are full of symbols. The *interpre-*

tations of the symbols are what make a prophecy either a clear vision, or an absurdity. Often prophets don't know what their own visions mean. One of the most famous prophecies of the twentieth century belonged to Jean Dixon. In her vision, she saw the White House as we might see it in a photograph, then she saw a black shroud drop over the image. Her correct interpretation of this symbol was her accurate prophecy of the assassination of President Kennedy.

Rapture comes from a Latin verb that means "to be seized", or "to be caught up."[45] Rapture is an experience attributable to seers and sages over the centuries that allows them to be witness to visions. More importantly, Rapture is very much associated with the last days. The Rapture is believed to occur at the end of the current, Church Age, and will be the inauguration of the Age of Tribulation.

Revelation generically refers to the disclosure of a higher power; a god/God communicating to a person or a people. Literally, it is the last book of the New Testament of the Christian bible, and the subject of countless discussions over the centuries. Is this most famous horror story in all of literature to be taken literally as a future that is unavoidable, or is it an allegorical tale? This depiction of the fate of mankind, and how it is understood, has much to teach us concerning our feelings about ourselves, and our perception of our destiny.

Tribulation literally means to "press hard upon", referring to grapes. It is commonly understood to mean oppression, anguish, and persecution.[46] Cultures under tribulation were likely to forsee an eschatological scenario which would liberate them from their circumstances.

So what sort of cultural consciousness could generate such dramatic eschatological scenarios? Chapter Two shall examine several groups and the harsh conditions in which they found themselves.

Chapter One Bibliography

1. Puhvel, Jaan. (1987). *Comparative Mythology* (p.1). Baltimore: The John's Hopkins University Press.
2. *Ibid.*
3. *Ibid.,* (p.2).
4. *Ibid.,* (p.2).
5. Bierlein, J.F. (1994). *Parallel Myths* (p.5). New York: Ballantine Books.
6. Campbell, J. (1969). *Primitive Mythology* (p.22). New York: Penguin Books.
7. Bierlein, J.F. (1994). *Parallel Myths* (p.5). New York: Ballantine Books.
8. Campbell, J. (1969). *Primitive Mythology* (p.22). New York: Penguin Books.
9. Ibid.
10. Rasmussen, K. (1927). *Across Arctic America* (p.82-84). In Campbell, J. (1969). *Primitive Mythology* (p.244). New York: Penguin Books.
11. Campbell, J. (1969). *Primitive Mythology* (p.54). New York: Penguin Books.
12. *Ibid.,* (p.57).
13. *Ibid.,* (p.244).
14. *Ibid.,* (p.57).
15. Jordan, M. (1993). *Myths of the World: a Thematic Encyclopedia* (p.55). London: Kyle Cathie Limited.
16. Campbell, J. (1969). *Primitive Mythology* (p.54). New York: Penguin Books.
17. *Ibid.*
18. Cotterell, A. (1986). *A Dictionary of World Mytholog.* (p.192). Oxford: Oxford University Press.
19. Eliade, M. (1954). *The Myth of Eternal Return* (p.113). Princeton: Princeton University Press.
20. Campbell, J. (1969). *Primitive Mythology* (p.54). New York: Penguin Books.

21. Eliade, M. (1954). *The Myth of Eternal Return* (p.113). Princeton: Princeton University Press.

22. Radice, B. (Ed.) (1973). *The Dhammapada* (p.44). Middlesex: Penguin Books.

23. Blackney, R.B. (Ed.) (1955). *Tao Te Ching: the Classic Translation.* New York: Mentor Books.

24. Eliade, M. (1954). *The Myth of Eternal Return* (p.51). Princeton: Princeton University Press.

25. *Ibid.,* (p.54).

26. *Ibid.,* (p.51).

27. *Ibid.,* (p.54).

28. *Ibid.,* (p.53).

29. *Ibid.,* (p.57).

30. *Ibid.,* (p.53).

31. *Ibid.,* (p.57).

32. *Ibid.,* (p.53).

33. Strozier, C. (1994). *Apocaplyse: on the Psychology of Fundamentalism in America* (p.5) Boston: Beacon Press.

34. Bierlein, J.F. (1994). *Parallel Myths* (p. xiii). New York: Ballatine Books.

35. Mann, A.T. (1992). *Millennium Prophecies* (p.72). Rockport: Element Books.

36. *Microsoft Encarta Encyclopedia* (1996). Antichrist.

37. Lorie, P. (1994). *Revelation* (p.8). New York: Simon and Schuster.

38. York, L.K. (1996) *History of Millennialism.*

39. *Microsoft Encarta Encyclopedia* (1996). Eschatology.

40. Campbell, J. (1969). *Primitive Mythology* (p.66). New York: Penguin Books.

41. Mann, A.T. (1992). *Millennium Prophecies* (p.12). Rockport: Element Books.

42. *Ibid.,* (p.12).

43. *Ibid.,* (p.13).

44. Reagan, D. (1996). *Amillennial Problems.* Lamb and Lion Ministries.

45. Doud, W. (1996). *The Rapture.*

46. Rhodes, R. (1996). *The Doctrine of the Tribulation.* Reasoning from the Scriptures Ministries.

Queen Katherine's Dream, William Blake.

Chapter Two

The End in Cultural Contexts

For the Osage Indians, it was the custom, when a child was born, to summon "a man who had talked with the gods," and when he reached the mother's house, he recited the creation of the universe and the terrestrial animals to the newborn baby. Not until this had been done was the child given the breast. Later, when the baby wanted water, the man, ...recited the creation of water. When the child was old enough to take solid food, the man... recited the origin of grains and other foods. It would be hard to find a more eloquent example of the belief that each new birth represents a symbolic recapitulation of the cosmogony [creation] and the tribe's mythic history.[1]

THE EARTH MOTHER

Mother Earth is a reference heard from time to time, most commonly in an ecological context. The term is used by people rightfully concerned about the compromised *life giving* ability of the planet. Such a reference is the modern version of an enduring recognition. As our ancient ancestors witnessed the miracle of both human and animal birth, or the simple but powerful beauty of mother nourishing child, it was easy to see the earth as maternal and nurturing, as well as a provider of almost infinite generosity.[2]

The earth appeared as a cornucopia or horn of plenty, the source of endless bounty. Animals, especially when observed exiting caves or burrows, seemed to be literally born of the earth. With the arrival of spring and the plentitude of the growing season, the earth mother seemed to be fully engaged in giving life and nourishment to humankind.[3] This abundance was the product of the simple act of depositing a seed into soil, which seemed to be the very body of the mother. The deposit of this apparently lifeless seed into soil resulted in a new life through the fecundity of the earth mother, who was the ultimate womb.[4]

This image was not without impact on our forebears. Over 200,000 years ago, someone or some group thought that the planting of lifeless human remains into the body/soil of the earth mother would result in *some* kind of new life.[5] Uncovered Neanderthal graves have revealed skeletons accompanied by supplies which have been buried in an east-west orientation, attentive to the rising and setting of the sun. Remarkably, the skeletons have also been placed in a womb-like/sleeping posture.[6]

It would be hard to describe the symbiotic relationship that our ancient ancestors experienced with the earth mother.[7] A contemporary counterpart exists only in those cultures labeled "primitive." In technological societies it is for the most part lost. But our forebears attributed the ultimate power of life to the earth-goddess; the responsibility for bearing life, and for destroying it.

MOTHER ENRAGED

Mother Earth provides a dichotomous circumstance for the life assigned to her. We have already mentioned her bounty, but she has also provided the stage for the catastrophes of nature that have impacted or destroyed countless lives. Over the centuries, how many people have been lost to earthquakes, floods, hurricanes, tornadoes, typhoons, tsunamis, volcanoes, or other natural disasters? Our ancient ancestors' observations of the vagaries of nature are among the most vivid and accurate historical records that we have. The fact that the awesome beauty and fecundity of the earth-mother is tempered by an absolute capacity for death and destruction is etched into our collective unconscious. It is a constant source of insecurity for people, regardless of culture. Life is a gift bestowed upon us by whatever power we may designate, and that same power can also retract that gift.

Any chronicle of nature will illustrate in the most violent terms the revocation of that gift of life. Blizzards, fire, drought: the awesome power of nature can be expressed in a variety of destructive nightmares. The myths of many cultures include the destruction of all existence (except for selected survivors) by flood, usually generated by God/gods to rid the world of beings marred by evil and sinfulness. Some notable flood mythological scenarios follow.

ANCIENT FLOOD ESCHATOLOGY

Flood symbolism appears in the creation and/or eschatology mythology of a variety of cultures. This mythology serves to describe the absolute origin of the world, or the recreation of the world following a cataclysmic, or millennial, event. Flood or water images are extremely powerful symbols, because they can represent both life *and* death. For our purposes, the importance of the water symbol lies in the promise of *regeneration,* the rebirth that follows death.[10]

In the waters we see the "reservoir of all the potentialities of existence,"[11] which represent the original form of the cosmos. The preform of the waters is often, throughout cultures, the manifestation of what existed before creation. A familiar creation image that will be illustrated in the following pages describes an island or mountaintop emerging through the formlessness of the waters. The appearance of form is the manifestation of existence and all its implicit promises.[12] This facet of water symbolism portrays water as the formless medium of pre-existence, whose recession is the precursor to the forms and shapes that contain existence.

There is also an alternate perspective to water symbolism. While the emergence from water depicts potential, *immersion* describes liquefaction. The formed becomes formless, as creation is dissolved into the primordial state. The important implication in reimmersion is the fact that it does not represent a destruction that is final and irreversible. It is a "temporary re-entry into the indistinct,"[13] that is followed by a new existence, or new creation. The reimmersion as a symbolic threshold to a new world or a new life is apparent in a variety of circumstances that are familiar to many of us.

One celebrated capacity of water as purifying is as part of the Christian ritual of Baptism. Baptism is the welcome and initiation into the spiritual community. Part of this process requires the washing away of sin. This process is most often conducted by pouring a small amount of water on the forehead of the Baptism candidate. However, for some groups, the process is conducted as described in the New Testament, meaning the candidate is completely immersed in a river or lake. In this immersion, sins are ritually washed away from the candidate's being. Other religions share this symbolism; Hindus ritually bathe in the sacred Ganges River, and Muslims cleanse their bodies in a short ritual before entering a Mosque for worship. In being reborn of the waters, whether literally, as when a mother's water breaks, or ritually, as in each of these examples, the gift of life begins. This commencement is a most celebratory event, but bears an advisement. As the waters recede, whether from the flood, from the mother, or from these rituals, the progression of time starts, unabated. Slowly but inexorably, age, wear, decline, and corruption augment their power. Cycles progress from their dawn to their dusk, until the time when a reimmersion is required, because the jagged edges of existence, honed by the imperfections of people, beg for the formlessness of the primordial waters.[14]

ATRAHASIS

This prominent epic of destruction by flood hails from Babylon/Mesopotamia. It was written about 1700 B.C.E. This story concerns *Atrahasis*, a name which translates as "extra-wise". *Atrahasis* was also the name of a pre-historical ruler in the area currently known as southern Iraq.[15] This myth tells of gods who are weary both from the toil of the creation of the world and the constant monitoring of the irrigation canals necessary to maintain life in Mesopotamia. Their dissatisfaction with their circumstances leads to a meeting among the gods. Ellil, the creator-god, is challenged by the lesser gods over their grievances.[16] Ellil hears their concerns and directs them to create mankind to assist them in their labors. Fourteen people are then created from clay mixed with the blood of a sacrificed minor god who, interestingly, is a god of intellect.[17] In the centuries following the creation, Ellil becomes incensed at the chaos generated by the burgeoning population below. In response, he orders the adjustment of the population through the natural forces he has at his command. The gods maximally obey Ellil's command, sending drought, famine, and disease so severe, that after some years, only a few people survive.[18] Dissatisfied that their destructive goals were not totally efficient, the gods prepare to send a flood to finish their task.

Atrahasis is secretly instructed to build a boat that would contain "the living things of the earth".[19] A flood follows that lasts seven days, and when Ellil hears that Atrahasis and his wife have survived, the god is outraged. He is persuaded by Enki, the god of wisdom, that humans can continue and, in the future, be regulated more with compassion than destruction.[20]

Flood mythology may be familiar to many because of their exposure to the Old Testament story of *Noah*, but *Atrahasis* shows us that flood mythology is much older than *Genesis*, part of which is the chronicle of the flood. *Atrahasis* may be as much as 5000 years old in its oral version. The age of this chronicle illustrates the fundamental aspects of flood eschatology. What is expressed is the dissatisfaction, even outrage, of the God/gods with the aftermath of their creation. Mankind, it seems, eternally sins, depriving the world of the luster and glow of the purity of creation. Freshness has gone; corruption has asserted its power. Through a flood, all that is tainted could be washed away, and humanity, wiped out except for those few spared, could start anew.[21] This is the cyclical aspect of eschatological thought, very common throughout mythology. In much the same way that days, seasons, and years have a beginning and an end, so does existence itself. The beginning is perfection; the end is chaos. This is the basis of millennial thought, and of many prophecies that exist to this day: *The corruption of the world requires its destruction by catastrophe, and its subsequent re-creation or renewal.*[22]

The notion of the flood is not the only scenario for the end of days. This 'flooded' end of the world reflected what was important to the cultures that drew these scenarios. What is uncertain is if there is an even older version of an eschatological deluge, and what its cultural origin might be.[23] The story of Atrahasis reflects the Babylonian view of the repeating cycles of an end leading to a new beginning, of chaos replaced by order. The Judaic-Christian account of the flood in *Genesis* is symbolic of the anticipation held by both traditions of the formation of a new order, one to succeed the extant, profane orthodoxy.

NOAH

According to the *Book of Genesis*, written about 1200 B.C.E., God's wrath at the world for its sinfulness was directed at all of the world's inhabitants except Noah, his wife, his three sons, and their wives. God gave Noah seven days notice to build a boat that would contain his family as well as one fertile pair of every animal specimen. Seven days later the rain began, and continued, according to tradition, for forty days. For one hundred fifty days after the rain stopped, there was nothing but water to be seen on the planet. God's anger subsided, so He sent a breeze to evaporate the water, and finally land emerges. Noah leaves the vessel with his family and the living things and makes a sacrifice, and God promises never to inflict a flood so massive on the earth again. This promise is sealed with the gift of a rainbow.[24] Noah went on, according to Genesis, to invent wine making, understandable after his adventure, and live to the age of 950 years.[25]

While flood eschatology seems unpleasant, since the world and its population are destroyed, the reader or listener is not assailed with the horrific images that are imaginable in a tremendous flood. The emphasis of the works steers toward the wonderful promise that can be fulfilled only after the deluge and repurification of the earth. The re-creation, the new order, the new existence are the focus. Literally adapted, there could be no movie-of-the week or blockbuster film generated by ancient flood mythology. But time, politics, the squalor over the advent of a new cult (Christianity), and the imagination of a writer borrowing heavily from his past would change eschatological temperament for many cultures over many years. With the *Book of Revelations*, eschatology was administered with a hammer, as the end of the world was transformed into a nightmare. Let's take a look at the Judaic roots of Revelations.

ISAIAH

Tanakh, the Holy Scriptures of the Judaic tradition, can be divided into three sections: the *Torah*, the five Books of Moses; the *Nevi'im*, the Books of the Prophets; and the *Kethuvim*, the Writings. The account of Noah comes from *Genesis*, the first book of the *Torah*. The *Book of Isaiah* is one of the books of the Nevi'im, or Prophets. The *Book of Isaiah* is reputed to have been written between 740 and 700 B.C.E. Interestingly, *Isaiah*, now over 2500 years old, survives intact. It was found hidden in an urn inside a cave above the Dead Sea in 1947. Could it be a deliberate metaphor that a scroll dictating death and destruction was found near the *Dead* Sea in an *urn*? Reputed to be the most ancient apocalyptic prophecy, this *Book of Isaiah* is now stored in a museum in Jerusalem in a facility designed to protect the scroll from a nuclear event.[26] It is grimly amusing that a document that predicts Armageddon has been protected from what many consider to be the means to that event. The fact that this book also purportedly predicts a nuclear attack on Jerusalem is an ironic matter that will be presented later in our discussion of the Bible Code.

As we discuss Isaiah, let us keep in mind that the torment in some of his visions is a reflection of the turmoil of his time, as is the case with many apocalyptic accounts. For Isaiah, the political and military events surrounding the Assyrian attack on Syria and Palestine mirrored the vengeance of a God outraged with the infidelity and sinfulness of his people.[27]

The *Book of Isaiah* opens with the pointed words of an angry God who feels that his children have rebelled against him. The words "evil and depravity" are used to describe the activity of the people, and their beings are described as full of "...bruises, welts, and festering sores..."[28] The world is observed to be a wasteland with cities burnt down; a place evocative of another Sodom and Gomorrah. Those with public responsibility are chastised for being rogues and consorting with thieves. Many of the actions of the people, God says in *Isaiah,* "...have become a burden to Me, I cannot endure them."[29] The twenty-fourth chapter of *Isaiah* presents the wrath of a deity that has simply been exasperated by his people. The earth, according to the text, is "...stripped bare, And lay it waste, And twist its surface, And scatter its inhabitants..."[30]

As Isaiah continues, it is explained that the defilement of the earth, the ignorance of teachings, and the breaking of laws and covenants have produced a curse that consumes the earth. The world becomes a place devoid of joy and gladness, and the very structure of the earth totters, breaks, and crumbles. In this dramatic portrait of creation chastised, Isaiah reminds us that even the sun and the moon are embarrassed and humiliated in the face of God. Kings will be punished and sent to a locked dungeon as captives. Cities and towns will be reduced to rubble, never to rise again. The thirty-fourth chapter of Isaiah can only be described as gruesome. God is described as "furious... at all the nations,...at all their host"[31]; in his fury, God resorts to carnage:

"He has doomed them, consigned them to slaughter.

Their slain shall be left lying.

And the stench of their corpses shall mount;

And the hills shall be drenched with their blood,

All the host of heaven shall molder.

The heavens shall be rolled up like a scroll,

And their host shall wither

Like a leaf withering on a vine

Or shriveled fruit on a fig tree."[32]

This chapter continues in an unrestrained indulgence of gory images of the great tribulation to come. Blood, fat, pitch, sulfur, crows, ravens, thorns, nettles, jackals, demons, snakes, and buzzards appear in only twelve verses! Isaiah balances this onslaught of darkness with the next chapter's depiction of the glories that God will save for the chosen.[33] The miraculous trappings include cures for the disabled and water flowing in the desert. Joy and gladness are to be the order of the day, in an existence where sorrow is absent. As Isaiah concludes, the Lord describes the characteristics of the New Heaven and the New Earth to come; a utopian existence, filled with images of long life, bountiful harvests, and peace. He dictates that the present world will not even be a memory: "The former things shall not be remembered, they shall never come to mind."[34] We shall see these images repeated shortly in the New Testament account of Revelations.

DANIEL

The Book of *Isaiah*, as we have said, is one of the Books of the Prophets. The Book of *Daniel* also deals with prophetic visions, yet is assigned to the *Kethuvim*, the Books of Writings. The fact that *Daniel* is not one of the premier, or even minor prophets of the *Tanakh*, is just part of the controversy surrounding this account. It is difficult to find agreement regarding the date *Daniel* was written, or even by whom. There is also concern about its authenticity and accuracy in depicting historical events. The authors of this text appeared to have used a technique called *vaticinia ex eventu,* or prophecy after the fact. The text is presented as the prophecies of *Daniel* in the sixth century B.C.E., but it was actually written four centuries after the events took place. Nonetheless, it is a fascinating work, and its prophetic images in Chapters 7- 12 deserve our attention. As with *Isaiah,* as well as many other apocalyptic works, *Daniel* was written in a difficult historical time, and depicts distressing events from the past.[35] In 597 B.C.E., Nebuchadnezzar had captured Jerusalem and imprisoned community leaders. Ten years later, Jerusalem was ravaged again, in a nightmare made real.[36]

In Chapter Seven, Daniel relates a dream that he records upon awakening. In his dream he sees four beasts emerging from the sea.

The first beast is a lion with the wings of an eagle; the second is like a bear, with three fangs in its mouth; the third appears to be a leopard, but with four wings and four heads; and the fourth beast had iron teeth, "that devoured and crushed, and stamped the remains with its feet... it had ten horns... with eyes like a man, and a mouth that spoke arrogantly."[37] Following this startling procession, the "Ancient of Days"[38] arrives on a throne of flame, with cloak-like garments white as snow[39] and a river of fire before Him. In His presence, the fourth beast is destroyed by the flames. The vision continues with the appearance of what is considered to be a prophetic vision of the coming of the Messiah/Christ, as well as the Anti-Christ. These images, although describing the political climate of the times in which the book was written, will come back to haunt us anew in another Biblical work.

The Eighth Chapter of Daniel describes another vision. A powerful ram stands beside a river, master of all that surrounds him, until the appearance of a goat, who strikes the ram and breaks the ram's horns. The horn of the goat is also broken, to be replaced by four horns. One additional horn grows so great that it knocks some of the stars from the heavens to the ground, which are then trampled by the beast. The text goes on to describe "truth hurled to the ground," and "a Holy place abandoned."[40] This a reference to turmoil during the sack of Jerusalem. Upon inquiring about the duration of the injustice against the heavenly host, he is answered "for twenty-three hundred evenings and mornings."[41] Daniel is advised by Gabriel that his vision "refers to the time of the end."[42] Daniel is further told "to keep the vision a secret, for it pertains to far off days."[43]

We have already discussed the self-deprivation that seers endured in order to facilitate their visions. In the Tenth Chapter of Daniel, we are witness to his ritual to achieve this effect:

"At that time, I, Daniel, kept three full weeks of mourning,
I ate no tasty food, nor did any meat or wine enter my mouth.
I did not annoint myself until the three weeks were over,
It was the twenty-fourth day of the first month,
  when I was on the bank of the great river, the Tigris,
  that I looked and saw a man dressed in linen, his loins girt in fine
    gold.

His body was like beryl, his face had the appearance of lightening,
his eyes were like flaming torches,
his arms and legs had the color of burnished bronze,
and the sound of his speech was like the noise of a multitude....
I alone saw the vision, ...I was drained of strength, my vigor was
    destroyed,
and I could not summon up strength."
Daniel 10: 2-8

The being is an envoy sent to Daniel, to praise him for his abstinence and to reward him with visions of what was yet to come.

In Daniel, Chapter Twelve, we are captivated by the scenario of a
time of tribulation. Resurrection is foretold, as those who "sleep in
the dust of the earth, will awake, some to eternal life, some to abhor-
rence."[44] The chapter, and the *Book of Daniel*, closes with a plea to
the Lord for a hint of when these terrible days might come. Daniel is
told "to keep the words secret, and seal the book until the time of
the end."[45] A twentieth century explanation of "the seal" that is fascinating will be presented in a later chapter. He is further instructed
to "go on to the end; you shall rest, and arise to your destiny at the
end of the days."[46]

The Book of Daniel is an exercise, by an undetermined author, to
explain the circumstances of one time (perhaps as late as 164 C.E. in
its final form), in the form of visions recorded centuries before (ca.
600 B.C.E.). This validation of prophecies provided reinforcement
for the faithful, as well as allowing the burdens felt by the contemporaries of the author to seem less onerous.[47]

The visions of Daniel, especially the vision of the four beasts, are
a view of the history of the era. The four beasts are the four king-
doms exercising authority over the people of Israel. Starting with
Nebuchadnezzer, through Alexander the Great, but especially with
the reign of Antiochus Epiphanes, these realms mark a degeneration
of existence, representative of a progressive threat to the very existence of the people of Israel.[48] We have witnessed the degeneration
of a particular society as a triggering episode for an eschatological
event. In the society's decay, a cycle draws to a close and begs for a
renewal, a rebirth, a recreation. But what is crucial in Daniel is not
that he has presented an original scenario, because he has not.

There are precedents for his symbolic imagery in Iranian, Babylonian, and Phoenician mythological traditions. [49] What begs our attention is that the Daniel vision transcends traditional cosmic cycles.

Daniel tells us that *God has a plan.* And in that plan, there are *chosen people.*[50] The chosen will be saved (Heaven help the rest of us). And with the introduction of this train of thought, Apocalyptic Literature is born, and the cycles of traditional mythology erode. Disintegration, decrepitude, and chaos withdraw as the governing factors of the destruction and regeneration of existence. A presence is noted, and mythologically, this presence is bequeathed power and and influence over history and events. This power, this presence, is called *evil.* Evil is personified by *Satan,* who although formerly a heavenly personality, carries a developed hostility to man, and more importantly, an adversarial relationship with God. The power of Satan is such that in this world, Satan is a profane god.[51] We need to note that as much as Satan is a harbinger of doom, his presence simply represents another cycle in another form. At the peak of his influence, the degradation of the world, another sequence/cycle will have been completed, chaos will reign, and the need for a return to order will be required.

What both Isaish and Daniel have shown us is that the Jewish apocalypse is fraught with horrendous events, to be followed by the resurrection of the dead and universal judgement. The implications of this were to be felt dramatically within the new cult of Christianity, not only in the first century, but for two millennia to follow.

REVELATIONS

In the centuries that have followed the death of Christ, the mission of Christianity to count its faithful in every corner of the globe has been, by any estimation, tremendously successful. In its dissemination worldwide, Christianity has utilized, as its principal instrument of communication and instruction, the Bible. Statistics vary, but at least one source indicates the distribution and sale of *nine billion* bibles in the last half-century alone. In addition, the Bible has been translated into 300 languages, and some individual books have been translated into 2000 languages and dialects.[52] This flurry of numbers is provided in order to account for the tremen-

Sean M. O'Shea and Meryl A. Walker

The Four Horsemen of the Apocalypse, Albrecht Dürer, 1498.

dous impact of the Bible, and most notably for our purposes, the New Testament, which concludes with the Book of Revelations. This apocalyptic scenario is certainly the most recognized in the largely Christian Western Hemisphere, but also enjoys notoriety throughout those parts of the world that have felt the impact of Christian missionary intervention. As the *Millennium Myth* continues, the reader will see that the *literal* interpretation of this scenario by a variety of Christian groups has found its way into world history, world affairs, and world politics.

The *power* that this last book of the Bible has upon large numbers of Christians around the world should not be underestimated. Please recall that 40% of the American public alone believe that the Bible is the *literal* word of God. And in the formidable impression that this eloquent text leaves with so many people, we find a view of the end of time that is simultaneously horrifying and intriguing. Moreover, it shares a familiarity, even an intimacy, with a large percentage of the populace. If many believe this scenario literally, how many more recall it as part of their upbringing, tugging at a religious tradition changed or abandoned? What is being suggested is that a majority of the population of the Western Hemisphere has an anticipation of a Millennial or Apocalyptic event. If not guided by overt religious fervor, then simple curiosity has many people wanting to know what to expect with the change of the century, and the change of the millennia.

The terms *Revelation* and *Apocalypse* are often used interchangeably, for good reason. The Greek term *apocalypsis* means a *revealing,* or a *prophetic vision.* Most often, this vision equates with *eschatology,* another Greek term which refers to the study of "last things."[53]

In the work of John of Patmos, we find the confluence of the three terms in their most prominent literary display.

John of Patmos, who would later be given the name St. John the Divine, was a disciple of Jesus Christ. The largest Gothic cathedral in the world, in New York City, bears his name. This wonderfully dynamic spiritual and cultural center is renowned for the fact that after more than one hundred years, its construction remains incomplete, generating the alternative name St. John the Unfinished. Construction continues, but local folklore indicates that when the cathedral is finished, the world will end.

It is important to note the political and social climate of the time in which John lived; primarily the fact that Christianity in John's time was a *cult.*[54] Perhaps a reminder of our reception and perception of some newsworthy contemporary groups might lend a perspective on how the original Christians were welcomed. There was an uncomfortable interface between an absolute power, Rome, and the impassioned members of a group whose leader, Jesus, had been their contemporary, and had achieved divine status. Rome perceived Christians as a threat to the social stability of the empire.[55] One of Rome's solutions was to remove this perceived threat, either by murder or expulsion.[56] In the late first century, John found himself exiled to the island of Patmos, in the Aegean Sea. Near the very end of the first century, between the years 49 and 95, tradition says that John was visited by an angel bearing a message from God, relating the contents of the *Book of Revelations.*[57]

What is immediately clear from reading the first lines of *Revelations* is that John's vision would become reality *soon.* There are no symbolic numbers of days or years for contention. John tells us straight: *the time is at hand.* In prefacing his visions, John uses the descriptor "when I was in ecstasy." Recalling the self-denial of Daniel and other seers of the past, one wonders about John's regimen to achieve his ecstatic state. From the beginning of *Revelations*, we are witness to John's influences in his writing. Images of the "Son of Man," with "hair white, with the whiteness of wool, like snow... his feet like burnished bronze..."[58] reminds us of the imagery of Daniel. The reminder comes again in Chapter Four, with the appearance of creatures commensurate with those of Daniel. In this same chapter, we are witness to the power of John's writing. Using the imagery of jewels, colors, and the forces of nature, he creates a scenario that is riveting, even two thousand years later, in a multimedia age. As Revelations continues to unfold, the might and majesty of God are described in terms that challenge the imagination. For example, the witnesses to the developments include angels. Not one, not one hundred, but ten thousand times ten thousand! While we cannot, for the purposes of this book, dwell on all the extensive symbolic representations to be found in *Revelations*, some symbols do require our attention. All symbols are subject to interpretations that vary with the observer.

The sixth chapter of *Revelations* presents us with the Seven Seals. The seals appear on a scroll, and are to be opened by the Lamb. The opening of the seals may imply that spiritual truth and enlighten-ment are difficult to obtain. The number seven appears throughout cultures as a number of significance, possibly because it signifies completion and order. The moon has four phases, each of which lasts seven days. For a long period of time the universe was thought to consist of seven planets. Babylonian, Buddhist, and Chinese tra-ditions all incorporate the significance of the number seven.[59] The Lamb is a traditional symbol of peace and gentility. Also, in its role of chosen sacrificial animal, the Lamb connotes Christ.

The seals are opened, and 'The Horsemen of the Apocalypse' appear. Any reader's reaction of "I've heard of this", is indicative of the cultural consciousness of *Revelations*, however removed. Even the association with Notre Dame football is part of this infusion, because even at the level of recreation, it communicates inevitabili-ty. The four horsemen of *Revelations* are the expression of the pri-mal fears of mankind, past, present, and forever.

War (the white horse), pestilence (the red horse), famine (the black horse), and death (the pale horse) are depicted as free to conduct their grim business with the breaking of their seals. What is sad about our existence is that these four horsemen have had the opportunity to ride unbridled throughout our his-tory. In the ever-ending story of the millennium, when have these curses been absent from our lives?

As *Revelations* continues, those who have been faithful to God are rewarded with His favor and protection from the coming horrors. With the opening of the seventh seal, there is absolute silence in heaven, which prophetic tradition holds to be the signal of the com-ing of the Lord.[60] Seven angels prepare to sound their trumpets. With the sound of the first trumpet, a third of the earth is destroyed by hail and fire mixed with blood. The sound of the second trumpet causes a mountain of fire to be cast into the sea, killing a third of all of the sea creatures, destroying a third of all ships, and turning a third of the sea into blood. The third trumpet sounds and a star named Wormwood falls from the sky. It turns one third of all drink-ing water so bitter that many die. Wormwood, by the way, is a com-mon Eurasian plant that yields a very bitter oil. When the fourth trumpet is heard, a third of the light of the sun, moon, and stars turns to darkness.

These images would not have been entirely new to the early audi-ence of Revelations. They would have made the connection between these horrors and the plagues that befell Egypt. In addition, they would recall that Old Testament prophets warned of the vengeance of God, who would certainly send scourges upon a faithless Israel.[61]

The sound of the fifth trumpet produces a plague of locusts of a most unusual kind. These were more like scorpions, because of their sting, and had the appearance of horses armoured for battle, as well as lion's teeth. Their direction was to attack and torture those who did not have God's seal on their forehead. Locusts are an ancient symbol of invaders, since they are literally seen as invaders of crops. Symbolically, they represent invading armies, not an uncommon historical circumstance in the experience and memory of the *Revelations* audience.[62] The sixth trumpet produces four angels leading an enormous army sent to destroy one third of the human race for their continuing sin.

The seventh trumpet produces a vision of a woman in childbirth threatened by a dragon. The birth is successful, and child and mother are protected by God. War breaks out in heaven, and the dragon and his followers are defeated and cast down to the earth. On earth, the dragon pursues the mother of the child, trying to engulf her in a river he spews from his mouth. He fails as the mother is once again saved. Enraged at his failure, he seeks revenge on her children. Here, John describes the faithful as the mother, always to be protected by God. The child represents the Messiah. The dragon is Satan, or the Roman Empire, seeking to engulf the followers of Christianity.[63]

In Chapter Thirteen, we encounter two beasts, one who emerges from the sea, the other who comes from the land. The beast from the sea is elaborately described as having seven heads and ten horns. The tremendous power of this beast comes from the dragon. The second beast comes from the ground and exercises his power on behalf of the first beast. This beast has the power to perform great miracles, and is marked with the number 666. The influence of these beasts over mankind is depicted as enormous. The first beast is symbolic of a false messiah, and probably represents the Roman Empire. The second beast symbolizes a false prophet; the infamous Anti-Christ. The number 666 corresponds to the letter values for the name Caesar Nero.[64]

The God's anger at the unfaithful continues in Chapter Sixteen. Seven angels, bearing seven golden bowls each filled with a plague, empty the bowls onto the earth. The first plague produces virulent sores, and the second plague turns the sea into blood, killing all the sea creatures. The next plagues turn drinking water into blood, scorch the earth, plunge the empire of the beast into darkness, dry up the Euphrates River, and cause earthquakes and hailstorms. Arrangements are made to gather armies at Armageddon.

The drying of the Euphrates River is written as a wishful thought against Rome. The Euphrates served as a natural barrier against the Parthian Warriors, who were perceived as a threat by Rome. Armageddon, now understood to imply a final battle, was in those times understood as a site of disaster for the armies gathering there.[65]

The end of Chapter Nineteen describes a battle fought between the forces of the Word of God and the forces of the Beasts. The Beasts are captured and thrown into a lake of flaming sulfur, and their warriors are all slain. Following this episode, the millennium begins. Chapter Twenty describes the imprisonment of Satan for a thousand years and the reign of Christ, joined by the resurrected just. Following the thousand-year period, Satan will be released from prison, mobilize for a war, which he will lose, and finally join the beasts in the sulfur lake to be forever tortured. The Last Judgement follows, with the remaining dead resurrected and the unjust also sent to the burning lake. A new heaven and a new earth follow, as does a new Jerusalem. At the end of *Revelations*, John is advised to spread the words of the prophecies, "...because the Time is close."[66]

In the *Book of Revelations*, we are witness to the definition of the genre of apocalyptic writing. The accounts that we have briefly explored thus far have all contained components of this style. These components include: the completion of a cycle, degeneration into chaos, the need for a new order, visions, the presence of evil, destruction, conflict, a messiah, and a new age to come. All of these components are revealed through the elaborate use of symbolism and metaphor. This imagery served several purposes. The writer, usually in a difficult political or social circumstance, could say what he was thinking in a way that could be understood by his intended audience, yet not directly enough to bring harm to himself. The message was enhanced by painting it in larger-than-life terms. Clearly there is a difference between "The Lord will come to save us", and "His throne was tongues of flame; its wheels were blazing fire..."[67]

In times of political duress, all that is left is a dream or a vision. The subjugation of a people by a power that appears insurmountable mandates an outlet, even if only a dream. Apocalyptic scenarios offer the promise of justice, a vision of wrongs undone, and a recreation of what is supposed to be.

What is sadly lost, is the intimate knowledge of the symbolism, the experience of the times, the actual meaning absorbed by the audience. We will never understand this work in the same way as the original listeners.[68] We can only interpret, which is at best an imperfect science. One is reminded of the line spoken following a poorly related story... "you had to be there."

There is a pervasive triggering mechanism that is related to both classic and contemporary eschatological scenarios. It is this mechanism that generates the ever-ending aspect to the millennium myth: *Crisis.* When has history ever been without it? When hasn't some group ever felt oppressed? Isn't it a fact that there has been less than a single year in all of recorded history when there has been no war? It is in the presence of the continuing oppression of groups, and in the continuing conflicts that we inflict upon one another, that we will always find someone looking toward a millennium to end the pain of their present condition. You may be surprised at how this has shaped world history. Following *Revelations*, we will take a look at the eschatology of some other cultures and see some interesting similarities as well as some different perspectives.

THE END OF THE KALI YUGA

In the preceding chapter, we discussed the importance of cycles. For our ancestors, cycles were the mechanism for "periodic regeneration through the annulment of time."[69] Cycles reflected a desire to return to the perceived perfection of the past; to an age of purity, to the unspoiled time of creation. We have seen this strongly and repeatedly illustrated in flood mythology, with the waters evoking the properties of cleansing, as well as primordial formlessness. In the dissipation of the flood, with land rising from the sea, the creation of a new order is accomplished. Cultures differed in their perception of time and cyclical regeneration. In the Indian/Hindu tradition, the recurring cycles of the universe are portrayed on a scale that flirts with infinity.[70]

In the Hindu tradition, cycles can be divided into their smallest components, called a *Yuga*, or an age. A *yuga* is preceded by a "dawn," and concludes with a "twilight." The dawn and the twilight are periods that connect one age to another, and each have a duration equivalent to one-tenth of a *yuga*. There are four world ages: *Krta, Treta, Dvapara,* and *Kali.* The complete duration of the four ages, including their twilight and dawn, is called a *Mahayuga.* The duration of a Mahayuga is 12,000 years, illustrated in numbers of years as follows:

YUGA	DAWN	DURATION	TWILIGHT	TOTAL
Krta	400	4000	400	4800
Treta	300	3000	300	3600
Dvapra	200	2000	200	2400
Kali	100	1000	100	1200

A Mahayuga is the total number of years in a cycle, which is: 12,000 years.[71]

There is, you will note, a pattern of decreased duration in the yugas. Moving from the Krta Yuga, the yuga closest to primordial perfection, each progressive yuga grows shorter and shorter, as chaos and decrepitude increase in prominence. The Krta (or Krita) Yuga is an age of grace and virtue in which people exist at their righteous best. This age appears to be utopian. The following age, the Treta Yuga, presents the familiar imperfections of humankind. The highest gifts of humanity are no longer instinctive, they need to be taught. Enlightenment is no longer inherent, it needs to be acquired through ritual. The Dvarpara Yuga is an age when virtue is in remission, and society is in disorder, riddled by "disease, desire, and disaster,"[72] as well as strife and discord. The final age, the Kali Yuga, our present age, is a shadow age where humanity sees the luster of its golden virtues darkened by the nightmares of our own creation: war, biological disaster, nuclear winter. The mystical union of love and sex is separated, confused, and transformed into the profane. Society determines that possessions, not spirit, are the barometers for prominence and leadership.[73]

At this point we venture into the flirtation with infinity that the Hindu tradition affords us. A taste of the tremendous view of time has already been illustrated in the portrayal of the ages. With each cycle being twelve thousand years, a Mahapralaya occurs at the conclusion of one thousand cycles, or twelve million years. There appears to be some disagreement on the actual meaning of time within each cycle.[74] Regardless of disagreement, the Hindu tradition deals with time in very large sizes. Some sources consider *each year* of the Mahayuga as a divine year.[75] A divine year lasts 360 conventional years. By this calculation, each Mahayuga lasts 4,320,000 years. Therefore, the time to the Mahapralaya, the great dissolution, is 4,320,000,000 years. But rather than concluding here, Hindu time calculation continues with a *Kalpa*. A Kalpa is one thousand Mahayuga. One Kalpa is measured as a day in the life of Brahma, the creator-god, another as a night. If your calculator is not handy, this means that a single day in the life of Brahma is 8,640,000,000 years. Brahma lives for a *Para,* as does the universe. A Para is a century of Kalpa days and Kalpa nights. Thus, according to Hindu tradition, the life of Brahma and therefore of the universe is 315,360,000,000,000 years or 315.36 trillion years. As we approach the year 2000, we find ourselves at the beginning of the last half of the para. At this writing, Brahma is about fifty years old.[76]

Whether seen in the simple recurrence of a day, or over the ages and eons spanning trillions of years, cycles dictate a millennial view of existence. Many cultures share the view that humanity starts in what seems to be utopian fashion, then becomes progressively less noble. At the point of chaos, the world and all existence requires termination, followed by the fresh start of creation.

Hindu eschatology is contained in their sacred texts, called *Puranas.* The *Puranas* translate as "stories of the old days."[77] Most of the *Puranas* were written around the year 500.[78] The end of the world, for the Hindu, occurs with the twilight of the Kali Yuga, the last of the four world ages. The end of the world, the Pralaya, will be repeated one thousand times. Finally, there will be the Mahapralaya, the great dissolution. The destruction of the earth becomes the task of Vishnu, a major god of Hinduism, and a very popular figure in Indian mythology. Sometimes referred to as the preserver of the universe, Vishnu is credited with having saved humankind on many occasions.

The great dissolution begins with the earth becoming a wasteland. A one hundred-year drought causes many to perish. Vishnu gathers himself to finish the task of destroying all of the earth's creatures. Through seven rays of the sun, all water is absorbed, streams, rivers, and oceans alike, to be consumed by Vishnu. Vishnu turns the seven rays of the sun into seven suns, which proceed to burn the earth so that it becomes as "bare as a turtle's back."[79] This is followed by a "tornado of flame"[80] which consumes all creation. Vishnu then creates clouds from his breath, which flash lightning and rumble with thunder. These clouds appear in the sky in a multitude of colors and shapes. When they have filled the sky, a tremendous rainstorm begins that extinguishes the fire engulfing the world. Rain falls for one hundred years, until the world is covered by a single ocean. Wind blown from the mouth of Vishnu takes one hundred years to dispel the clouds. At the end of the period of dissolution, Vishnu takes the form of Brahma so that a world can be created once again, and cycles start anew.[81]

RAGNAROK, THE TWILIGHT OF THE GODS

Cultures see their own apocalypse in scenes and images familiar to them. Since myth is a mirror reflecting the culture in which it was born, the content of such myth is a statement of the hopes and fears of a people. In apocalyptic myth, we find an itemization of a people's greatest fears, frozen in the time of the myth's origin. In addition, we may find it to be an allegorical description of the social and political climate of a particular era.[82]

Norse mythology documents the beginnings and the end of a world age in an epic poem called the *Voluspa,* or Sibyl's Prophecy. With origins estimated at the year 870 C.E.[83], the *Voluspa* describes the origin of the gods, with Odin the most prominent of all. Odin's existence begins when he is freed from the ice by a lick of Audhumla, a cow formed from primordial mists. The earth is created when Odin slays Ymir, a giant of enormous proportion, with his spear. Ymir's carcass becomes the earth; his blood the oceans; and his hair the vegetation. The spilling of Ymir's blood is so tremendous that some of the undesirable, lesser giants of existence are drowned.[84] Clearly, this represents the Norse version of the flood purging existence so that the select may start their new order.

The *Voluspa* also chronicles the final chapter of the world. Ragnarok, the Twilight of the Gods, is the Norse apocalypse. It is interesting not only for its similarity to the *Book of Revelations* in its imagery of the destruction of the world, but in the fact that the victims of the conflagration include the gods themselves.[85]

The tribulations begin with three successive winters unbroken by summer. During these winters, warfare engulfs the entire world. In the course of these wars, brother will kill brother and incest will proliferate. This will be followed by three more winters unbroken by summer. However, these last three winters will be of the harshest variety ever known, with unparalleled intensities of snow, frost, and winds.[86]

In the continuing nightmare of Ragnarok, the sun and the moon, chased by the wolves of the heavens since creation, are finally caught and consumed by these beasts. The stars disappear as well, and darkness prevails. Neither trees nor mountains remain standing, because the earth quakes with an unimaginable violence. All things bound are freed, as all restraints are broken.[87] The great wolf Fenrir was tricked into bondage by the gods, who feared his great strength. Fenrir breaks free of his massive chains and is free to act out his rage toward the gods who deceived him.[88] Fenrir's liberation finds him racing across the cosmos with his massive jaw gaping, eyes blazing with rage. So formidable is this beast that his upper jaw reaches the top of the sky, with his lower jaw on the surface of the earth; he stands shoulder high to the gods.[89]

With all restraints broken, Naglfar, the ship of the dead, is now free of its moorings. Naglfar is the grisly vessel constructed from the nail parings of the dead. Our image of tenth century Vikings, with long hair and full beards, sailing for months on end fiercely waging war, does not include fastidious grooming. Yet for whatever tonsorial failings they might have had, their nails were cut so as to avoid completing the construction of this apocalyptic ship, and postpone its maiden voyage as long as possible. It would be this ship that would carry Loki, a giant possessed of wit, intellect, and evil, and Hrym, a leader of the frost giants, to Vigrid, the site of the gathering for the final battle. In the growing chaos and horror overtaking the world, the Midgard Serpent is furiously seeking to leave the churning sea to get ashore. It is ultimately successful, and appears with hosts of others at Vigrid. This serpent will proceed to spew poison upon the skies and seas.[90]

The stage for the final battle is set with the gathering at Vigrid. The skies themselves are torn and warriors ride through them to be joined by the family of Hel, the goddess of the underworld. The gods are summoned by the sound of a horn. At this time fear was so great throughout the universe that even Yggdrasil, the cosmic tree previously mentioned, trembled.[91, 92]

In the ultimate engagement that follows, Thor, the son of Odin, kills the Midgard Serpent, but is himself killed by the serpent's poison. Odin is also killed, swallowed by Fenrir, who will also be killed during the battle by the god Vidar. In a final horror, the world is consumed by flames sent by Surt, the spirit of fire.

In its benevolence and justice, the Norse universe retains realms for existence. Brimir and Sindri are the names of the halls where the good will dwell. Among the amenities to be found in these halls are good drink and a rich ambience provided by red gold. On the other hand, the evil will find themselves on Nastrandir, which contains a hall constructed from the backs of serpents and renowned for its horror. Torrents of serpent poison run throughout the hall, enveloping the evil inhabitants. Vicar and the other remaining gods dwell in Asgard, where the former house of the gods existed. The earth will rise anew from the sea, and be green and fertile. Two survivors will proceed to fill the world with people, and the sun's daughter will copy her mother.[93] The saga ends with the conclusion of Snurri Sturluson, the thirteenth century Icelandic scholar responsible for the retelling of the *Voluspa*. "An idllyic age will ensue, and all shall live in love."[94]

In Ragnarok, we find a powerful apocalyptic vision, reminiscent of *Revelations* in its sheer horror. The seer who constructed this scenario knew his people well. Carved into this account are the fears of a people who live in a climate that is only benevolent for half the year. The forces of ice and frost play major roles in this epic, as they did in the daily lives of the people. Frost was such a force that it was personified in this myth as a group of giants. Ice is powerful enough as to deny existence to Odin himself until the intervention of the warm, life-giving lick of Audhumla.

The precursor to Ragnarok is the very frightening prospect of successive winters unbroken by summer. Powerful roles are also assumed by wolves, creatures that were a source of trepidation. In this myth they take on the unimaginable size and prowess that not only equates them with the gods, but allows them to swallow the sun, the moon, and the gods themselves. The elimination of light was a powerful stress for a people whose fear of a darkness lasting months was very real.

Ragnarok is reputed to have been composed around the time of Viking expansion and the progress of Christianity into the northern reaches of Europe. Its origin during this period of extreme violence may explain the backdrop of this saga, born in a universe awash in the blood of the giant Ymir, and resolved in the bloodbath on the plain of Vigrid, the Twilight of the Gods.[95]

Whether it be the spread of Christianity, as we have just seen, or the threat to Christianity, as we saw with *Revelations*, there is usually a social or political triggering mechanism that causes a millennial fervor. Following our look at eastern religious traditions, some of those events will be explored.

Chapter Two Bibliography

1. Eliot, Alexander (1976). *The Universal Myths* (p. 28). New York: Meridian Books.

2. Campbell, J. (1969). *Primitive Mythology* (p.66). New York: Penguin Books.

3. *Ibid.,* (p66).

4. *Ibid.,* (p.66).

5. *Ibid.,* (p.66).

6. *Ibid.,* (p.67).

7. *Ibid.,* (p.67).

8. *Ibid.,* (p.68).

9. *Ibid.,* (p.68).

10. Eliade, M. (1991). *Images and Symbols* (p.151). Princeton: Princeton University Press

11. *Ibid.,* (p.151)

12. *Ibid.,* (p.151)

13. *Ibid.,* (p.152)

14. *Ibid.,* (p.152)

15. Jordan, M. (1993). *Myths of the World: a Thematic Encyclopdia* (p.36). London: Lyle Cathie Limited.

16. *Ibid.,* (p.37).

17. *Ibid.,* (p.37).

18. *Ibid.,* (p.37)

19. *Ibid.,* (p.37).

20. *Ibid.,* (p.37).

21. Eliot, Alexander (1976). *The Universal Myths* (p. 29). New York: Meridian Books.

22. *Ibid.,* (p.30)

23. *Microsoft Encarta Encyclopedia* (1996). Deluge.

24. Jordan, M. (1993). *Myths of the World: a Thematic Encyclopedia* (p.109-110). London: Lyle Cathie Limited.

25. Cotterell, A. (1986). *A Dictionary of World Mythology* (p. 40). Oxford: Oxford University Press.

26. Drosnin, M. (1997) *The Bible Code* (p.121-122). New York:

Simon and Schuster.

27. Eliade, M. (1978). *A History of Religious Ideas. Volume 1* (p.347-348). Chicago: The University of Chicago Press.

28. Isaiah, 1:6.

29. Isaiah, 1:14.

30. Isaiah, 24:1-2.

31. Isaiah, 34:2.

32. Isaiah, 34: 2-4.

33. Isaiah, 35.

34. Isaiah, 65:17.

35. Cotterell, A. (1986). *A Dictionary of World Mythology* (p. 23). Oxford: Oxford University Press.

36. Ibid.

37. Daniel, 7: 7-8.

38 Daniel, 7: 9.

39. Jordan, M. (1993). *Myths of the World: a Thematic Encyclopedia* (p.109-110). London: Lyle Cathie Limited.

40. Daniel, 8: 11-12.

41. Daniel, 8: 13-14.

42. Daniel, 8: 17.

43. Daniel, 8: 26.

44. Daniel, 12:1-2.

45. Daniel, 12:4.

46. Daniel, 12:12

47. Eliade, M. (1978). *A History of Religious Ideas. Vol. 2* (p.265). Chicago: The University of Chicago Press.

48. *Ibid.,* (p.265-266).

49. *Ibid.,* (p.266).

50. *Ibid.,* (p.266).

51. *Ibid.,* (p.269).

52. United Bible Society.

53. Leeming, D.A. (1990). *The World of Myth* (p. 76). New York: Oxford University Press.

54. Lorie, P. (1994). *Revelations* (p.15). New York: Simon and

Schuster.

55. *Ibid.*

56. *Ibid.*

57. *Ibid.*

58. Revelations, 1:14.

59. Lorie, P. (1994). *Revelations* (p.85-86). New York: Simon and Schuster.

60. *The New Testament of the New Jerusalem Bible* (p. 507) Garden City: Image Books.

61. *Ibid.*

62. *Ibid.*

63. *Ibid.,* (p. 508).

64. *Ibid.*

65. *Ibid.,* (p. 509).

66. Revelations, 22:11.

67. Daniel, 7:9.

68. *Microsoft Encarta Encyclopedia* (1996). Revelation.

69. Eliade, M. (1954). *The Myth of the Eternal Return* (p.85). Princeton: Princeton University Press.

70. *Ibid.,* (p.112).

71. *Ibid.,* (p.112).

72. Cotterell, A. (1986). *A Dictionary of World Mythology* (p. 94). Oxford: Oxford University Press.

73. *Ibid.,* (p. 94-95).

74. Eliade, M. (1954). *The Myth of the Eternal Return* (p.114). Princeton: Princeton University Press.

75. *Ibid.*

76. Cotterell, A. (1986). *A Dictionary of World Mythology* (p. 94). Oxford: Oxford University Press.

77. Leeming, D.A. (1990). *The World of Myth.* (p. 81). New York: Oxford University Press.

78. Jordan, M. (1993). *Myths of the World: a Thematic Encyclopedia.* (p.115). London: Lyle Cathie Limited.

79. *Ibid.,* (p.83).

80. *Ibid.*

81. *Ibid.,* (p. 84).

82. *Ibid.,* (p.107).

83. Eliot, Alexander (1976). *The Universal Myth.* (p. 72). New York: Meridian Books.

84. *Ibid.,* (p.73).

85. *Ibid.,* (p.157).

86. Leeming, D.A. (1990). *The World of Myth* (p. 86). New York: Oxford University Press.

87. Ibid.

88. Eliot, Alexander (1976). *The Universal Myth.* (p. 157). New York: Meridian Books.

89. Leeming, D.A. (1990). *The World of Myth* (p. 86). New York: Oxford University Press.

90. *Ibid.*

91. *Ibid.,* (p. 87).

92. Cotterell, A. (1986). *A Dictionary of World Mythology* (p. 193). Oxford: Oxford University Press.

93. Leeming, D.A. (1990). *The World of Myth* (p. 87-88). New York: Oxford University Press.

94. Cotterell, A. (1986). *A Dictionary of World Mythology* (p. 174). Oxford: Oxford University Press.

95. *Ibid.*

Chapter Three

The Millennium in Eastern Religious Tradition

"The life of humanity upon this planet may yet come to an end, and a very terrible end. But I would have you notice that this end is threatened in our time not by anything that the universe may do to us, but only by what man may do to himself."[1]

THE HINDU TRADITION

The *Hindu tradition* deserves honor for a variety of reasons; among those is its very vastness. Hinduism acknowledges all of the needs of those driven to worship. Whether those requirements are of simple animism, which is the veneration of the elements found in nature, to the most complicated hierarchial system of deities, there is room in Hinduism for all. There are in Hinduism, literally, millions of objects, personas, and deities for homage.[2] With such a vast number of opportunities for spiritual exercise, Hinduism is completely tolerant of human spiritual need. In much the same way that Sanskrit, the original language of Hinduism, has been called the mother of languages, Hinduism has a maternal role in the propagation of other religions, most prominently Buddhism.

While having no founder that we can identify, nor a figure we can revere in his/her authorship or revelation of a seminal text, Hinduism has not been without renowned historical figures.[3] In this century, Gandhi, a Hindu ascetic, was instrumental in the movement of India from British colony to independent democracy. A figure of international stature, he was given the name *Mahatma,* Sanskrit for *great soul.*

The history of the Hindus begins at the Indus River valley in India. In the third millennium B.C.E., an already extant civilization was thriving, but over the next millennium, it would go into decline. There is not much known about these Indus Valley inhabitants, except that their decline allowed nomadic groups to settle in the same area.[4]

By the end of the second millennium B.C.E., history records the arrival of nomadic groups called the Indo-Aryans, or Aryans. *Aryans,* a Sanskrit term for *the noble ones,* did not represent a single tribe or people. They were represented by a diverse membership including peoples from as far away as Europe, as well as the more immediate vicinity of Asia. Hopfe, in his thorough examination, *Religions of the*

The Empyrean, Gustave Dore

World, cautions us against applying the twentieth century perception of the term Aryan to this ancient historical settlement. These Aryans were not a single race, nor a master race, and therefore should not be confused with the twisted vision of a twentieth century dictator.[5]

Over time, the settlements grew and societal organization began to take shape. Leadership was assumed by *Rajas,* and a class of priests called *Brahmins* was established. What we now understand as the caste system began to establish its roots.[6] This new society worshiped many deities, who were associated with the natural events that were prominent in the lives of the settlers. Among the various rites practiced in Aryan worship was sacrifice. While sacrifice was common for people of this era, the Aryans undertook this ritual expansively.

Hopfe reports that the Aryans practiced sacrifice in the most ostentatious form ever recorded. One ritual was called the horse sacrifice. Its tremendous expense confined its exercise to rulers, who sought to make reparations to the gods for a perceived sin, or more politically, to expand their territory. The horse chosen for this ritual was allowed to roam freely for a year. During that time it was followed, and all the land covered by the horse was annexed by the ruler. At the conclusion of the year, the horse was then sacrificed. Hopfe tells us that in addition to the horse, as many as *six hundred* other animals were sacrificed as well "ranging from the bee to the elephant."[7] Tradition dictated that one hundred such sacrifices would make the ruler lord of the universe. Time and expense, apparently, prevented that from ever happening.[8]

THE HINDU SCRIPTURES

The sacred scriptures of the Hindus are called the *Vedas,* which some sources date to before 2000 B.C.E. The word Veda translates as *knowledge* or *sacred lore.*[9] The Vedas were created in the media of hymn and poetry, before the gift of writing had been devised, and were celebrated, shared, and passed from one generation to the next. Prominent among the gods celebrated in the texts is Indra, the ruler of heaven, and the force behind the clouds and the rain. He is celebrated most notably for the vanquishing of Vrtra, the very embodiment of evil.[10]

The Vedas are divided into four books. The primary text is called the *Rig-Veda.* This text represents an anthology of over one thousand hymns to the Hindu deities. The basic Hindu mythology is contained in this book. The subsequent book is called *Yajur-Veda,* which translates as *knowledge of rites,* referring to sacrifice to the gods. The next book is the *Sama-Veda, the knowledge of chants,* also relating to sacrifice. The final book is the *Atharva-Veda, knowledge given by the sage Atharva,* which concerns itself with home practices, as well as methods to dispel evil.[11]

Each of the four Veda books is divided into four parts, with the final section of each called the *Upanishads.* The Upanishads are the philosophical narratives of the Vedas. Although part of the Vedas, the Upanishads are from a later time, probably the first millennium B.C.E.[12] The Upanishads also differ from the rest of the Vedas in that they distinctly convey monotheism, in the image of a being called *Brahman.* Hopfe tells us that Brahman exceeds being, he is the one reality. Outside of Brahman, there is no reality. Our existence, however we regard it, is distinctly illusion. Brahman is "without a past, present, or, future; and totally impersonal."[13] Additionally, the Upanishads differ from the Vedas by promulgating worship not through sacrifice, but rather through meditation. The Upanishads teach that we are ignorant, and must accept that, for only through this acceptance can enlightenment and knowledge be attained. This tall philosophical order is not one easily absorbed, and accounts for the resistance of these constructs by the masses.[14] But as we will see, these constructs will be popularized by an offspring of Hinduism called Buddhism.

The word *Karma,* which translates as *to do* or *to act,* is familiar to many of us and finds its origins in the Upanishads. In traditional Hindu thought, it was felt that each act or thought had a significance that would become apparent in either this life or one to follow. The admirable qualities that we observe in others in our lives are simply the product of their positive discretions in the past. The same holds true for evil manifestations.[15]

Another familiar Hindu concept for many of us is *reincarnation.* Popular literature, as well as our contemporary language, holds references to reincarnation. In the course of conversation, it is not uncommon to hear people refer to "a former life" to explain their actions, or those of others. These assertions are colloquial adaptations of the Hindu concept of *samsara,* which means to *wander across.*[16] At the end of life, the essence of an individual wanders across to another existence in another era. Often, and mistakenly, in the Western mind, this concept is seen positively, even with excitement, as the fulfillment of a wish shared by many. How many times have we expressed the desire to experience life anew, hoping, that with a second chance, the errors and heartaches of this life might be avoided.

However, in the Hindu mind and subsequently in the Buddhist

mind, the ongoing, even infinite repetition of life cycles is seen as a curse. In the Hindu tradition, life without enlightenment is nothing more than an illusion. The key is to live this life as best one can, and to seek enlightenment to break from this potentially eternal illusion; the endless repetition of the sequence of Karma, of life. This desire for enlightenment is called *moksha,* freedom from life.[17] In Hinduism, life is but a dream.

THE MAHABHARATA

In addition to the Vedas, the Hindu tradition has also left us with the *Mahabharata.* Scholars refer to the Mahabharata as an epic poem. We are probably most familiar with the term *epic* through motion pictures; a name that might come to mind is that of Cecil B. De Mille. Renowned for his productions such as *Ben-Hur* and *The Ten Commandments,* he told stories that were both larger than life, yet reflective of life, at the same time. But before the age of movies, epics were well established, in the literature that was ensconced in a variety of cultures. We have seen the scenarios painted by the authors of *Revelations* and *Ragnarok. The Aeneid, The Odyssey,* as well as *Paradise Lost* might come to mind as well. Epics, then, are portrayals depicted on exalted scale, of circumstances of pivotal importance, involving heroes and gods, on a landscape that may be as large as the universe itself. If length is any measure, the Mahabharata may be the most grand epic of all time. The longest epic in the literature of the world, with *90,000* verses, its complete form dates from the sixth century B.C.E.[18]

The Mahabharata is a poem that depicts the differences, and finally, the confrontation, between two family lines, both descendants of the Bharatas. One family was the Kurus, the other was the Pandus. The eldest of the Kurus, Duryodhana, has the blind king Dhrtarastra for a father. Duryodhana was not at all a nice person. He was consumed with hate for his cousins, the Pandus, with a hate so powerful he was regarded to be the incarnation of Kali, the demon of the dark age of the world, which happens to be our present world in Hindu tradition.[19]

Pandu was the younger brother of Dhrtarastra, and is represented in this epic by his five sons: Yudhisthira, Arjuna, Bhima, Nakula, and Sahadeva. The death of Pandu marks a transition period in which Dhrtarastra assumes leadership of the kingdom until

Yudhisthira comes of age to take the throne. Duryodhana busies himself by trying to kill his cousins by burning their home. The Pandus, the victims of this atrocity, escape to the forest unharmed. Upon discovering that the brothers are alive, Dhrtarastra gives them half of the kingdom. Yudhisthira accepts an invitation from Duryodhana to a game of dice and loses his kingdom, since one of the dice is loaded. Dhrtarastra, as king, reverses the outcome and allows the brothers to keep their kingdom. In addition, he allows another game to occur, which Yudhisthira loses again. As per the rules of the game, Yudhisthira and his brothers must give up their kingdom and live in exile in the forest for twelve years. At the end of the period of exile, the brothers demand the return of their kingdom, which is denied by Duryodhana. The hostility between the families peaks, and the specter of war grows as both sides begin to amass great armies.[20]

An eighteen day war follows, which the Mahabharata narrates in detail. The battlefield is littered with the dead. Duryodhana is one of the last to fall. The god Shiva, the destroyer, enters the fray by possessing one of the Kurus. He brings with him swarms of demons, who proceed to slay all of the Pandus save for the five brothers. Years after the great battle, death and destruction stalk the principal players of the Mahabharata. Dhrtarastra is killed in a sacred fire of his own making, and the Pandu brothers die one by one, on a trek to the Himalayas. The kingdom is reduced to rubble and collapses into the ocean. Only Yudhisthira survives, leaving his legacy to his grandnephew Pariksit, who was resurrected from death at birth by Krishna. Yudhisthira journeys to the underworld and then ascends into heaven.[21]

Within the Mahabharata is the *Bhagavad Gita,* perhaps the most notable part of this epic, and certainly the best known outside of the Hindu world. While the Mahabharata itself was created over an extensive period, the Bhagavad Gita came at the later part of that period, perhaps as late as the third century C.E.[22] The Bhagavad Gita takes place as the apocalyptic war between the Kurus and Pandus is about to start. Arjuna, a young warrior, is overcome by the incipient war, and ponders the very nature of war and all its horrors. He considers the possibility of entering the battle without weapons, and therefore committing suicide. What follows in the text is a discussion between Arjuna and his charioteer, Krsna (Krishna).

Krishna, upon hearing what Arjuna is considering, suggests that his idea would be acceptable were he not of the warrior class. As a warrior, however, he must do his warrior duty.[23]

The Bhagavad Gita teaches the obligation to duty that is required in order to free oneself from the karma of infinite cycles of birth and death. In addition, it portrays the god Vishnu, in the guise of Krishna, the charioteer, as a deity of utmost compassion and genuine love for humans. The promise of Vishnu in this text, to make himself available to humans in times of dire need, is poignantly comforting.[24]

The Mahabharata is a depiction of the end of the world, followed by the promise of a new world led by the resurrected Pariksit. Its themes of a great war, the conflict of good and evil, and death and destruction, were not new even to this ancient tradition. But, Eliade says, the Mahabharata tells this oft-told tale in the medium of dazzling poetic beauty.[25]

ZOROASTRIANISM

A simple way of measuring the significance of a religious tradition is by the simple estimation of the number of adherents. The major religions of the world today calculate their followers with eight, nine, and ten digit numbers. We are about to discuss a tradition, Zoroastrianism, that today has approximately 250,000 followers.[26] But as we will see, its historical legacy and influence on the infancy of what are now the major religions of Christianity, Judaism, and Islam, qualifies Zoroastrianism as a tradition of note.

Zoroastrianism may be as much as three thousand years old, and because of its age, details on its origins are both vague and in dispute. Zoroastrianism shares its inception with the Hindus. All the nomadic Aryans of that time did not settle in the Indus River valley. Some settled in the area east of Mesopotamia, and became the forebears of the people that we now refer to as Persians, who would go on to develop a great empire. Among the sources that tell us about these people are the *Gathas,* the hymns of the early Zoroastrians, which are believed to be the words of the prophet Zoroaster himself. The Gathas describe the Aryans as being similar to the Indus Aryans: worshipers of deities commensurate with the forces of nature that were observed, respected, and feared. Prominent among these gods was *Mithra*, the god of light, and provider of cattle. His popularity was such that the people would not allow him to be supplanted in the religious reform that was to come. He was simply included in the scenario, as the god of judgement.[27] The supreme deity, however, was *Ahura Mazda,* meaning *the wise lord.*

As with the Hindus, blood sacrifice was a common form of worship. In addition, for religious purposes, the juice of the haoma plant was consumed, probably for its hallucinogenic properties. The Aryans also believed in the presence of prophets. These figures, called *Saoshyants,* meaning *those who benefit the community,* were thought to appear when religious fervor was at an ebb. The greatest of these was Zoroaster.[28]

ZOROASTER

The birth date of Zoroaster is unclear. Estimates range from as early as 1400 B.C.E. to as late as 600 B.C.E. Born as Zarathustra Spitama, (latinized as Zoroaster) he was part of a warrior family connected to the royal family of Persia. In the details of his life, it becomes hard to separate fact from legend, as it is with any religious figure.[29] In fact, his life parallels that of another religious leader, Jesus Christ, in a number of areas. In infancy, Zoroaster's life was threatened because he was regarded as a threat, but he was saved through the intervention of higher powers. At the birth of Christ, tradition tells us that he was visited by the Magi, adherents of the god Mithra, during a time when the idea of a messianic king was being promulgated.[30] When Zoroaster's childhood drew to a close, he participated in the ritual that marked his passage into manhood. At the age of thirty, he began to assume his religious leadership, which was replete with visions, wandering, and a call to preach that there was one God, who for Zoroaster was Ahura Mazda. Finally, although Zoroaster lived much longer (age 77) than Christ, both were murdered at the hands of enemy soldiers.

PRINCIPLES OF ZOROASTRIANISM

Zoroaster's assertion that there was one god, Ahura Mazda, with the exclusion of the existence of all other gods, cannot be overlooked as insignificant. Many of us accept monotheism as part of our tradition, without a second thought. However, in the time of Zoroaster, this thought was considered revolutionary. Hopfe asks us to consider Moses, who *may* have been a contemporary of

Zoroaster. Moses preached to his followers that there were no other gods before YHWH, but never with the preclusion of the existence of other gods.[31]

The god of Zoroaster, Ahura Mazda, is referred to as "Him", but is not really a male character. Zoroaster depicted Ahura Mazda as having six modes, each representing the outstanding qualities of the god. Since the essence of supreme deity is by definition beyond the comprehension of mortals, Ahura Mazda can perhaps be more readily absorbed by individual attribute. Of these six attributes, three are considered male and three are considered female, hence, a god of balance.[32] This balance is further depicted in the notion of good and evil. Just as male and female qualities emanate from Ahura Mazda, so do spirits of good and evil. Co-existing since the beginning of time, the spirit of good, *Spenta Mainyu*, struggles with *Angra Mainyu,* evil. They meet in the totality of Ahura Mazda.[33]

Central to Zoroastrianism is the concept of free will. Born without sin, we are free to make the choices that will serve either good or evil, and do so without excuse. Our destiny, however, depends upon our choices, because in Zoroastrian eschatology we are ultimately responsible for all our choices.[34]

According to Zoroastrianism, after death, the soul remains with the corpse for three days, in order to contemplate the choices that were made in life. On the following day, the soul faces Mithra, who weighs the deeds of life on a scale. The evil are assigned to hell, and the good are escorted to paradise, a realm of beauty and light. Zoroastrian hell is a horrible place where the unfortunate are punished in accordance with their sins. Snakes protruding from bodily orifices, and the forced consumption of human discharge might give the reader some perspective. Sexual taboo is taken very seriously in Zoroastrianism.[35]

On a more positive note, Zoroastrian eschatology provides for a happy ending. At the end of days, the evil will be purified, and their souls will join those of the good. A new world cycle will commence, evil will be absent, and Ahura Mazda will reign forever.[36]

JUDAISM

Judaism is one of the oldest religious traditions in the world, and in that role shares an orientation with Christianity and Islam. But the followers of Judaism, Jews, are unique in a number of respects, which will be explored in depth. The history of Judaism is founded in God's disappointment with mankind. The Book of Genesis recounts the failure of Adam and Eve, the first murder in the interaction of Cain and Abel, and ultimately, God's need to recreate the world through the flood survived by his designee, Noah. The repeated failures of his human creation left him with no option but to choose a people with whom he could communicate and construct a pact, or covenant, that would bind them to a set of beliefs in exchange for his predisposition toward them. And the person that he chose, above all others, was Abram, later called Abraham.[37] Abraham represents the commencement of both Judaic and Islamic history.

It is unknown if Abraham was, in fact, a historical figure. Records that are available, however, indicate that his name and nomadic lifestyle are consistent with what is known about the area of the Fertile Crescent in the second millennium B.C.E. Other known details about this place and period indicate that the patriarchs of the Jews were apparently monotheistic, worshiping the God named *El.* This deity was worshiped through animal sacrifice on altars in open spaces.[38]

Having chosen Abraham as the leader of his people, God promised him a homeland for those people. It is in the struggle to attain that homeland that we find the story of the Exodus, the most important event in Judaic history.[39] The Exodus, as we know, is the narrative of the efforts of the descendants of Abraham, the Israelites, to break the bonds of Egyptian slavery, and journey to the promised land of Canaan. It highlights the communication between the God, YHWH, and Moses, the chosen leader of the Israelites. YHWH affirms his covenant with the people he has chosen, by intervention in human events, and delivering on his promise to Abraham to provide a homeland for his people. With the attainment of Canaan, the union of a people and the achievement of a collective goal was firmly entrenched in a communal psyche.

JUDAIC ESCHATOLOGY

The research conducted for this book revealed the eschatological traditions of many religions and cultures, both prominent and obscure. It was surprising, however, that the eschatological literature of such a prominent tradition such as Judaism was not as easily accessible as those of other religious or cultural orientations. Furthermore, the references that were available were vague.

In his book *Jewish Views of the Afterlife,* Raphael affirms the enigmatic, if not unique, perception of what Judaism esteems in the relationship, and relative importance, of the present life and what is purported to follow in the world to come.[40] As an illustration, Raphael relates a story of an elderly Jewish woman, well into her eighties, who was near death. In an attempt to comfort her mother in this difficult passage soon to be taken, her daughter plans to read her excerpts from the *Tibetan Book of the Dead.* A consulting psychologist with expertise in the dying, was familiar with the daughter's espoused text, and was concerned that the readings might confuse or even frighten the patient. As an alternative, Yiddish love songs were suggested.[41] The point that Raphael is trying to make is that contemporary Jews, even those well immersed in their culture and heritage, may be unaware of Judaic afterlife and eschatological traditions.

Some religions depict this life as one of preparation for the life that is to follow. The literature of the group defines optimal behaviors and attitudes to be emulated, as well as personal sacrifices to be assumed in the present life. These thoughts and activities become a kind of spiritual currency to be accumulated over one's lifetime, to be exchanged at death, or the apocalyptic moment, for participation in the awesome rewards that have been lavishly depicted for the righteous. This life then, in some religious conventions, is seen as a vehicle of denial, with the focus on the world that is to follow, where pleasure and enjoyment are sanctioned.

Judaism sees this world somewhat differently. For Jews, this life is a gift from God, a notion that is taken quite seriously. As a gift, life is to be enjoyed, celebrated, and savored in its sanctity, while fulfilling the special covenant they share with God and honoring his commandments. Such *this worldliness* might seem to preclude a substantial literature on the life to follow, but that is not the case. The literature and tradition are there, but as Raphael indicates, they seem to have been "lost" to many Jews for several reasons.[42]

As recently as the last century or so, there has been a dramatic change in the location of Jewish society. A number of forces, political as well as social, have seen Jews in large numbers displaced from their collective, traditional existence in the ghettoes of Europe and appearing in North America, where most of the world's Jews now live. This transition has been a significant one, because the European cultural enclaves of Jews, where Hebrew, Yiddish, and heritage thrived, have been replaced by the multi-cultural, multi-ethnic, English dominant America. Regardless of the tenacious intent of a people to cling to their customs, more often than not the price of assimilation is an altered legacy.[43]

Any consideration of the Jewish perspective on the afterlife or the world to come must consider the implications of the Holocaust in Jewish thought and feeling. Even to a people whose history has been scarred by repeated persecution and murder, the Holocaust, the systemized attempt of a country to render Jews *extinct,* has had an incomprehensible impact. In the face of apocalyptic death, one answer was to attend to life for those remaining, to ensure the existence of a people in *this* world. The consideration of the post-mortem fate of six million people is just too sad for contemplation.[44]

OLAM HA-BA

Seventeenth century Jewish tradition produced two texts that deal with the events that follow death. One is called *Maavor Yabok,* which means *Crossing the River Yabok.* The title refers to Jacob's crossing of the river Yabok in a story in Genesis. It is collection of writings on dying, death, and a depiction of the afterlife. It can be considered The Jewish Book of the Dead, and remains in print to this day. The other text is *Nishmat Hayyim, The Soul of Life*, written by Rabbi Menasseh ben Israel, a scholar and statesman of historical note. This book is a collection of Jewish beliefs on the soul, death, judgement, and reincarnation. Sections of the text are said to be the dictation of a *Malakh*, an angel.[45]

The collectivity of the Jewish people, so entrenched in Jewish thought, carries over to beliefs about the circumstances that follow this life and world. In this heritage is the term *Olam Ha-Ba, The World to Come*. While it can refer to an individual's life after death, it has also been used to describe the world of the promised messiah, the world of the new age of the Jewish people.[46] The medieval scholar Moses Maimonides describes Olam Ha-Ba as a place of happiness that is beyond our comprehension. What makes the Olam Ha-Ba of Maimonides so interesting is that there is nothing to be said about it. In contrast to the fabulous portrayals found in the eschatology of other orientations, Olam Ha-Ba is beyond description, assessment, or understanding in human terms. Perhaps it explains a part of the distance between Jews and their eschatological tradition. Such an ultimate concept may not have been worth much contemplation, especially when there were other spiritual and secular issues that required immediate attention.[47]

This concept of regard, or even honor, of the ultimate by saying as little as possible about it, reminds one of the Jewish tradition of reference to God. So beyond the human existence was this God that the application of a simple name to this being was inappropriate, for names were labels given to the material. Phrases such as *He who is,* were used in order to avoid the insult of human familiarity.

In the sacred texts of some religions, there is no question of meaning. For example, in Islam, as we shall see, the ecstatic experiences of Muhammad and the writings that have resulted from these interactions with the divine, are literally accepted. There is no interpretation of the *Koran.* What is written *is.* This is not so in Judaic literature. There is much that is open to discussion and review. Therefore, what is known about Olam Ha-Ba is not confined to the view of Maimonides. Rabbinic texts, some dating from the second century B.C.E., are not so descriptive about Olam Ha-Ba itself as they are about who will share in it. Among those to be excluded were the men of Sodom, and those denying the resurrection of the dead.[48]

Descriptions of the world to come include illustrations of a utopian *Olam Ha-Zeh,* meaning *this world.* In the world to come, for example, a single grape will yield thirty measures of wine. But more importantly, Olam Ha-Ba is the final exoneration of the people of Israel, the response of God to the past oppressions, persecutions, and injustices of history, as well as those that the writers could not have foreseen.[49]

Integral to the concept of the world to come is the notion of divine judgement. This notion has a variety of aspects, depending on the source. Upon the arrival of Olam Ha-Ba, individual judgement is indicated, as well as the judgement of the entire nation of Israel. And as the nation of Israel is judged collectively, so will other nations be judged. The Talmudic text *Avodah Zarah,* depicts the judgement of Rome and Persia. Appearing before God, they are filled with self-praise over their worldly advancements. Architecture and art, as well as political and military achievements are listed exhaustively. These national resumes are rejected, however, because of their collective failure to follow the *Torah, the law,* and the nations are condemned.[50]

AFTERLIFE REALMS

Judaism has a number of afterlife realms in which the dead were gathered in its tradition. The most prominently mentioned in non-Jewish literature, albeit vaguely, is *Sheol.* In the history of Jewish literature, Sheol has experienced some transformations which we will briefly explore. Originally, Sheol was simply a place for the dead to go. It was not characterized by good or evil, and interestingly, existed beyond the supervision of YHWH. YHWH was at this time the God of the living Israelites, and purportedly directed exclusively in their issues.[51] Perhaps Sheol is best described as an equivalent to the Greek mythological Hades, not a place of judgement, but a sad place nevertheless, because its inhabitants were devoid of the gift of life.

The inhabitants of Sheol, over time, were assigned the name *rephaim,* which can be translated as ghosts, or *powerless ones.* Interestingly, rephaim has another reference. In ancient Hebrew myth, before the Flood, there was a race of giants of the same name that were reportedly sentenced to destruction by God, and subsequently assigned to the underworld. As Judaic tradition progressed, the term rephaim was employed to refer to any resident of the underworld, hence, Sheol.[52]

Nefresh, the energy of life, the force of existence, the state of being; it is what separates the living from the dead. It is what we enjoy in life, what ebbs in sickness, and what depletes in death. This absence of life's energy is what characterized the sadness of the Sheol residents in Judaic tradition.[53] The conception of Sheol as a neutral haven of the dead was about to undergo a transformation relative to that of YHWH.

YHWH, the God of the nation of Israel, was originally a supreme, but not an exclusive deity. The pagan god Baal, for example, did not escape the attention, nor the worship, of the Israelites. Over time, however, the nation of Israel adopted a monotheism that discarded other gods, and enhanced the powers of YHWH. Sheol became a place of punishment, especially for those nations described as the enemies of Israel.[54]

Apocryphal literature, in reference to the afterlife realm of punishment, used another term that was synonymous with Sheol, *Gehenna.* Gehenna was, in fact, according to rabbinic texts, one of the primary constructs of the creation scenario. It was the place in the afterlife reserved for those who did not follow the Torah, engaged in the worship of idols, practiced incest, adultery, or lost their tempers. Gehenna was avoided by the simple practice of good deeds, such as sharing one's good fortune, tithing, and humility.[55]

Originally, Gehenna was not depicted as a place of everlasting torment. In contrast to the Christian portrayal of everlasting hell, Gehenna had a sentence of twelve months. It was a period of transition to purification, of the purgation of the sins accumulated during a lifetime. While other sources portray Gehenna as having a much longer duration for unfortunate souls, it is generally understood to be an impermanent residence.[56] Gehenna would appear to be commensurate with the later Christian concept of Purgatory. Gehenna is depicted, in various accounts, as a place of fire, brimstone, hail, snow, and darkness.[57]

More pleasantly, rabbinic literature also refers to *Gan Eden,* the Garden of Eden. Texts are unclear as to the attainment of Gan Eden, whether it be at the end of a righteous life, or at Olam Ha-Ba, the end of the present era. Thirteenth century texts describe Gan Eden as the location of delight, a land of flowers, milk, honey, and wine.[58]

Even in Gan Eden, there is a special place above all others. *Otzar,* or *divine treasury,* is the domain of the collection of the spirits of the virtuous. It is a depository of sorts, a gathering place of souls awaiting birth. *Tzror ha-hayyim* is the alternative name given to the warehouse of souls. Translated as *the bundle of life*, it is the state of being with God, the place which souls inhabit, awaiting the inspiration of God before returning to their next birth in Olam Ha-Zeh.[59]

BUDDHISM

Buddhism is the foremost child of Hinduism. Its origin was in the sixth century B. C. E. in India, under the tolerant cloak of its mother religion. Three centuries later, its appeal was such that it was encouraged to spread its message through the use of missionaries, a method previously unheard of in Hinduism. History would find this to be a fortuitous occurrence, because while the Asian communities of China, Korea, and Japan, among others, would embrace the

Buddhist practice, it would eventually be suppressed in its home-land of India.[60] The appeal of Buddhism, however, would endure, eventually finding a home even in America.[61]

Buddhism was founded by a man named Siddhartha, a member of the family called Gautama.[62] He is reported to have been born in 558 B.C.E., the son of a king, Suddhodana. He left his palace at the age of twenty-nine, and experienced his "awakening" at the age of thirty-five. He spent the rest of his life preaching, and died at the age of eighty, in 478 B.C.E.[63] These facts are reported as historical, as much of the other details of Siddhartha's life are assigned to legend, as is typical of any religious leader.

At his birth, it was predicted that Siddhartha would become either a ruler of prominence, or a great religious leader. In an effort to avoid the latter, Siddhartha's father shielded his son from the miseries of existence, and correspondingly, immersed him in the beauties of life. Despite his father's efforts, however, Siddhartha eventually witnessed the realities of life, having death, disease, and old age finally revealed to him. With the realization that outside of his privileged existence in the palace, life for most was pain and suffering, he left the comforts of the palace to find the meaning in life's misery.[64]

The answers to the questions that Buddha had about life were not forthcoming in philosophical study, in which he was immersed for a time, so he became an extreme ascetic. He willfully participated in the unpleasant, hoping to find release. He fasted until he was skeletal and actively sought discomfort and pain. For example, he sat on thorns, and slept among corpses.[65]

Deciding that asceticism was not the route to enlightenment, Siddhartha ate, and meditated under the shade of a tree. After a period of meditation, enlightenment came to him. He became known as *Buddha,* or *The Enlightened One.* Buddha's meditation revealed to him that the seemingly endless succession of birth and death experienced by humans was the product of the slavery of desire. He saw that he himself was the victim of desire, in his search for enlightenment. When he no longer desired enlightenment, it came to him. Buddha would spend the rest of his life as a teacher of his Four Noble Truths, as well as The Middle Way, avoiding the extremes of both pleasure and asceticism. All people of all classes were welcome to follow the way, differentiating Buddhism from the caste conscious Hinduism.[66]

Central to the teachings of the Buddha are the The Four Noble Truths. The First Noble Truth is *all is suffering.* The trauma of birth, the inevitability of age, the frailty of our bodies and our feelings, the heartaches associated with love, and the final descent into death are all forged in suffering. Even in happiness, or spirituality, there is suffering, simply because these desired states do not last.[67]

The Second Noble Truth depicts the source of suffering. *Tanha,* or *thirst,* is the pursuit of three varieties of desire: sensual pleasure, self perpetuation, and self destruction. The Third Noble Truth declares that the extinction of desire produces the end of suffering, and *nirvana,* the state of the Buddha, is attained. The Fourth Noble Truth describes how suffering might be conquered. The method by which this can be accomplished is called *The Middle Way,* or *The Eightfold Path.* The Middle Way, as we have said, seeks to avoid the extremes found in the pursuit of pleasure, or the denial of extreme asceticism. The Eightfold Path refers to a style of being that can alleviate suffering. It teaches right opinion, right thought, right speech, right activity, right means of existence, right effort, right attention, and right concentration. Ethics, discipline, and wisdom are the goals of the Buddhist practice, on a foundation of love and compassion for all.[68]

BUDDHIST COSMOLOGY

Among the interesting aspects of Buddhism, is the fact that Buddha never considered himself to be a prophet or the personal representative of any god. In fact, Buddha rejected the idea of a supreme being. What renders him divine was his desire for the deliverance of mankind.[69] Buddha refused to discuss cosmology, because for him the world was not the creation of a god, or an evil entity. For the Buddha, the world simply *is,* created and recreated in an ongoing fashion by the deeds of men, both good and evil. The proliferation of evil and ignorance succeed in shortening life, and dissipating the universe. Eliade relates the story of a monk who sought to elicit from Buddha, either answers to questions about the nature of the universe, or Buddha's admission that he did not know. In response, Buddha tells the story of a man shot with a poisoned arrow. When a physician is brought to him, the man refuses treatment until he discovers who shot the arrow, where that man lives, what family he is from, what kind of bow was used, who made the arrow and so on. Before the man could discover the answers to these many questions, he dies. Buddha's point was that some questions are not useful; a person can waste their whole life trying to know the unknowable, instead of enjoying what they do know. It is, he told the monk, more useful to spend time leading a holy and spiritual life than to wrestle with philosophical questions that may never be satisfactorily answered.[70]

Nonetheless, in the time after Buddha's death, an extraordinarily elaborate cosmology was constructed. We have already briefly described the expansive Hindu perspective on time and the universe. Buddhist cosmology is even more complicated, and employs numbers that flirt with infinity. Its complexity is such that there is relatively little literature on the subject, with only a few scholars boasting expertise in the area.

In the century following the Buddha's death, Buddhism split into two schools, and in the subsequent three centuries, these two schools became twenty. These schools are referred to as Abhidharma Buddhism. In the last century before the Common Era, a movement in reaction to Abhidharma Buddhism arose. It was called Mahayana Buddhism, and this movement would develop its own cosmology.[71] In our brief review of Buddhist cosmology, we will refer to the Abhidharma Buddhist tradition.

The Sanskrit term for *universe* is *loka-dhatu.* Its existence is assigned to the *karma*; the deeds and corresponding results of men. The universe is maintained by karma, and can dissipate by karma as well. By the third century of the Common Era, it came to be believed by Buddhists that the entire universe existed solely as a figment of the human imagination.[72]

The parameters of the Buddhist universe are enormous, and it is measured in a unit called a *yojana,* believed to be the equivalent of seven kilometers. The universe is described as a wind circle suspended in space. It has the shape of a disk, and is ten to the fifty-ninth power yojanas in circumference, a number called a novemdecillion, and is 1,600,000 yojanas deep. On the wind circle rests a water disk, substantially smaller in size and half as deep. On top of this rests the disk that is the earth, the same size as the water, but less thick.[73] A noteworthy feature of the earth is the presence of Mount Sumeru. Sumeru originated in the Mahabharata, hence it was another example of the Hindu origins of Buddhism. Mount Sumeru is assigned a height of 560,000 kilometers, and in its enormity is the backbone of the world. No part of the universe is free of its presence, as it pierces all layers. It is the very center of all existence, with four sides corresponding to the four directions. Each side is constructed of a different precious material. On the north it is made of gold, in the east, of silver, lapis lazuli on the south, and crystal on the west.[74]

In the Buddhist view, *Tri-dhatu,* or *all existence,* had levels, all of which were inhabited by some form of beings. The highest level, the level of formlessness, was inhabited by gods. The level of form was the home of lesser gods. We humans inhabit the surface of the earth, and beneath us are the demons and inhabitants of the hells.[75]

Niraya means *devoid of happiness,* and is a descriptor for the condition of hell. In Buddhism there are a series of hells, not just one as in Christianity. Among other descriptions, hell is portrayed as the place reserved for those who defame the teachers of The Way, or Buddhist practice. The duration of the stay is described as very long periods of time, and given the Buddhist proclivity to employ numbers, this was information that needed to be taken very seriously.[76]

Borrowing once again from its Hindu mother, Buddhism adopted a vision of hell that was painfully graphic. As was the custom in Buddhism, the eight "hot" hells are given specific dimensions in yojanas. Descriptions paint scenarios of torture and death by way of blades, a process that is repeated over and over. Dismemberment, agony, and heat are among the tortures of the different hells. Victims of passion are put through the process of chasing maidens up and down trees with leaves like swords, endlessly lacerating themselves. This process, according to one source, is repeated *ten trillion times.* Those guilty of crimes against children are forced to witness similar atrocities against their own children, and finally must endure the pouring of molten copper through their orifices.[77]

In addition to the hot hells, there are eight cold hells. These hells emphasize the tortures that are commensurate with extreme cold. The name of one of these hells is *Arbuda,* or *abscess,* describing the effect of extreme cold upon the skin. To this day the Japanese call pockmarks *abata,* a derivation of this term. Other cold hells have oddly poetic names. For example, *Utpala,* or *blue lotus, Padma,* or *red lotus,* and *Mahapadma,* or *deep red lotus.* The poetic charm of the names ebb, however, upon learning that the colors describe that of skin splitting due to varying degrees of extreme cold. Buddhism depicts 144 hells in all, including the hells of isolation. What is sadder, or more horrible, than being tortured alone?[78]

The balance of existence requires a counterpart to the image of hell, which is, of course, heaven. And as there are a plethora of hells in the Buddhist universe, so there are numerous heavens. The uppermost heaven is 162,772,160,000 yojanas from the earth layer. The foremost occupant of this realm, *Akanistha*, a deity, has other formidable attributes that need to be noted. Texts note his height as 16,000 yojanas, and his life span as 16,000 great kalpas, and since a great kalpa is eighty kalpas, his life span is 1,280,000 kalpas.[79] A kalpa, as we saw previously in Hindu literature, is twelve million years. But in Buddhist cosmology, a kalpa is expressed more abstractly than numerically. Sadakata tells us that it is the period required to wear away a rock one cubic yojana in size by wiping it with a piece of cotton once every century.[80]

As we descend from the uppermost reaches of the heavens, we encounter deities that gradually decrease in stature, and have life spans that ebb away from the infinite, but are nonetheless extensive.

Samsara, or *transmigration,* is the term assigned to the endless cycle of life, marked by birth and demise in our illusory world. In a fashion similar to individual beings, the cosmos itself also experiences samsara, although over much longer periods of time.[81] Samsara is a reflection of the pessimism that is inherent in Buddhist thought, because the sentence of repeated lives is seen as abhorrent. Buddhist conceptions about time correspond closely with our own notions of seconds, hours, days, months, and years. For periods longer than a year, we have mentioned the great duration of the kalpa and the great kalpa. As vast as these periods are, there is the even greater period of time called the *asamkhya kalpa*. This period, sometimes understood to mean infinity, is assigned an actual number, ten to the fifty-ninth power. We have previously seen this number assigned to the circumference of the Buddhist universe. Three asamkhya kalpas are the period of time required to train to become a buddha.[82]

The Buddhist cosmological cycle had four periods, with each lasting twenty kalpas. This eighty kalpa period begins with the Kalpa of Dissolution, followed by the Kalpa of Nothingness, the Kalpa of Creation, and the Kalpa of the Duration of the Created World. The Kalpa of Dissolution commences when the punishment of those in hell ceases and the occupants are reborn into heaven. When the hells eventually become unoccupied, they vanish from existence. In balance, rebirth in the heavens increases, as others are motivated to be reborn there. Once everyone is reborn into heaven, the world becomes ultimately vacant of the beings whose illusion is responsible for its creation. Seven suns then appear to vaporize the world. This dissolution is completed in the following Kalpa Of Nothingness.[83]

A new set of living beings, whose origin is unclear, recreates the universe through their karma. Over time, samsara and karma fill this universe once again with beings. During this period, the life span of beings is infinite. The following era is that of the Kalpa of Duration. In this Kalpa, human life spans decrease in correspondence with their collective commission of evil. War, pestilence, and famine are a part of this era. With a life span of less than one hundred years, we are presently seen to be in a period of decrease, and should expect a great famine to occur, as well as continually decreasing life spans.[84] We are living in the time of the *evil world,* where corruption is rampant, and beings are seen as so spiritually inferior, that we cannot even anticipate the arrival of another Buddha, because we are too dark of spirit, and too narrow of mind, to even benefit from his teachings.[85]

ISLAM

We have explored the great religious traditions of Asia, based upon their approximate date of origin. Islam is the last of these because it was established, relatively speaking, much more recently. Its origins date from the seventh century of the Common Era, and in the modern age enjoys a billion faithful, predominantly from the Middle East, Africa, and Asia.[86] The Islamic faithful worship only *Allah,* the supreme being of the universe. Allah revealed his wishes most fully to the prophet Muhammad in the seventh century. Allah required, through Muhammad, that his followers submit to his will in this life - the only life that was to be granted to them. The followers of Allah and His message are called *Muslims,* which translates as *submitters.*[87]

One of the benefits of the relatively recent arrival of Islam is the fact that we have access to accurate historical accounts of his existence. Muhammad ibn Abdallah[88] was born in Mecca between 567 and 572 to the powerful clan of the Quraysh. Later legends regarding his birth are commensurate with that of other outstanding religious figures. His mother is reputed to have been aware, through inspiration, that her son would be a great leader of his people. His birth was greeted by a light that shone throughout the world, circumstances that recall the phenomena surrounding the births of Zoroaster, the Buddha, and Jesus Christ.[89] The place of Muhammad's birth, Mecca, was a religious center even in pre-Islamic times. Derivations of the name *Mecca* translate as *sanctuary*. In the middle of this sanctuary, the *Ka'ba*, or cube, could be found. It was a building with an opening to the heavens that enclosed the Black Stone, which is believed to have come from the heavens.[90] It is probably a meteor.[91]

Muhammad and his contemporaries were immersed in the Judaism and Christianity practiced in their vicinity. There was an Arab resistance to Christianity, founded in the climate of the times. One source of dissatisfaction was that of dogma. There was much debate during this time over what was the exact relationship between God and Jesus Christ, as well as the mistreatment of the Arabs at the hands of Byzantine rulers. As a result, the message of a single God brought by a prophet with empathy toward the Arabs found an accepting audience.[92]

In his nomadic travels as an adult, Muhammad repeatedly encountered Jews, Christians, and Zoroastrians. His perception told him that all shared a similar eschatological view, with commensurate depictions of reward of the righteous and condemnation of the evil. What the fate of his own people might be was the source of much thought by Muhammad. During these thoughts, Islamic tradition reports, the prophet was visited by the angel Gabriel.

Gabriel brought from God the revelations that would be recorded in the form that we now know as the *Quran,* the sacred scriptures of Islam. His experiences with the divine taught Muhammad that he was the last of a series of prophets that included Abraham, Moses, and Jesus.

What is unusual about Islam is that it does not assign inferiority to other faiths. Islam sees itself as a finished product, with its forebears as concepts. Interestingly, Muhammad saw himself as only a prophet. He never deigned himself as divine.[93] In fact, Muhammad was very much a prophet in the Hebrew tradition; he was not divine, simply the messenger of a vision.[94]

Muhammad experienced many difficult days, as is the case with any new preacher of a new message. In addition, his beloved wife Khadija would predecease him, as would his protector, Abu-Talik. But word of Muhammad's principle would spread, and he would become a judge to settle disputes. In the year 622, Muhammad would leave Mecca, to journey to Medina to assume a role as a judge. His arrival at Medina, on September 24, 622, marks the *Hijrah,* or *migration,* and is the date from which the Muslim calendar is measured.[95]

A development worth noting transpired between Muhammad and the already established Jews of Medina. The monotheistic Jews clashed with the growing Islam. In response, Muhammad forbade his followers to pray toward Jerusalem, opting toward Mecca instead; an edict that lasts until this day.[96]

By 629, Muhammad was a force to be respected, and by 630, he had Mecca under his influence. At the Ka'ba, or Kaaba, Muhammad supervised the destruction of the idolatry depicted within, and became the unequivocal leader of the Arab people.[97]

Each religion has its own sacred text, as we have seen through our examination of varying traditions. The Quran, which is translated as *reading,* or *recitation,* is different from the Bible on one crucial point. The Bible, for many Christians and Jews, is a treatise that invites variant perception to its meaning. The Quran, on the other hand, is considered a verbatim text. Muslims consider it to be completely literal. For Muslims, what the Quran says is what it means. Muhammad was, although illiterate, the vehicle of the *exact* message of Allah. His memorization of these messages was then dictated to Zayd, Muhammad's secretary, who then wrote down these messages.[98] The Quran is the assembly of 114 chapters, referred to as *surahs,* which contain approximately 6,000 verses called *ayas.* The Quran is equivalent in size to the New Testament of the Bible. There is a tradition in Islam of committing the entire Quran to memory. Those who do so are given the title of honor, *Hafiz.*[99]

ISLAMIC ESCHATOLOGY

Eschatologically, Muslims see Allah as the judge of all men at the end of time. The impact of interactions with Jews, Christians, and Zoroastrians were not lost on Muhammad as he viewed the world to come. Upon the death of an individual, according to Islamic tradition, the body dies and the soul is immersed in sleep until the assigned date of resurrection. Upon this date, soul and body will be reunited. Allah will preside over all, judging adherence to the Quran. Followers of the Quran will be rewarded, with those resistant to the message doomed. Both heaven and hell await the judged, depending upon the quality each singular life passed. For the good, pleasures await, including those of water and shade, most attractive to residents of the desert. Additionally, there is the prospect of wine, normally forbidden to Islamic adherents. It is, in eschatology, totally non-intoxicating. Other attractions include thornless plants, trees laden with fruit, and lofty couches upon which the bliss of being chosen can be comfortably absorbed.[100] For the evil, a realm of distaste, especially for the desert nomad, is depicted as a place of winds propelled by heat, ensconced by smoke, and filled with waters that are foul and unrefreshing.[101]

Having briefly explored the apocalyptic scenarios of a number of prominent religious traditions, we will now witness the power of the beliefs in these images in the context of selected historical events.

Chapter Three Bibliography

1. Holmes, J. H. (1933). *The Sensible Man's View of Religion.* In Bartlett, J. (1980). *Bartlett's Familiar Quotations.* (p. 765). New York: Little, Brown, and Company.

2. Hopfe, L. (1994). *Religions of the World.* (p. 76). Englewood Cliffs: Macmillan College Publishing Company.

3. *Ibid.*

4. *Ibid.,* (p. 80).

5. *Ibid.*

6. *Ibid.*

7. *Ibid.* (p. 81).

8. *Ibid.*

9. *Ibid.,* (p. 82).

10. *Ibid.,* (p. 83).

11. *Ibid.,* (p. 82).

12. *Ibid.,* (p. 83).

13. *Ibid.,* (p. 87).

14. *Ibid.*

15. *Ibid.,* (p. 88).

16. *Ibid.*

17. *Ibid.,* (p. 89).

18. Eliade, M. (1982). *A History of Religious Ideas: Volume Two: From Gautama Buddha to the Triumph of Christianity.* (p. 232). Chicago: University of Chicago Press.

19. *Ibid.,* (p. 232).

20. *Ibid.,* (p. 233).

21. *Ibid.,* (p. 233-234).

22. Hopfe, L. (1994). *Religions of the World.* (p. 95). Englewood Cliffs: Macmillan College Publishing Company.

23. *Ibid.,* (p. 96).

24. *Ibid.*

25. Eliade, M. (1982). *A History of Religious Ideas: Volume Two: From Gautama Buddha to the Triumph of Christianity.* (p. 235). Chicago: University of Chicago Press.

26. Hopfe, L. (1994). *Religions of the World.* (p. 246). Englewood Cliffs: Macmillan College Publishing Company.

27. *Ibid.*

28. *Ibid.,* (p. 247).

29. *Ibid.,* (p. 246).

30. Eliade, M. (1982). *A History of Religious Ideas: Volume Two: From Gautama Buddha to the Triumph of Christianity.* (p. 307). Chicago: University of Chicago Press.

31. Hopfe, L. (1994). *Religions of the World.* (p. 249). Englewood Cliffs: Macmillan College Publishing Company.

32. *Ibid.,* (p. 250).

33. *Ibid.,* (p. 251).

34. *Ibid.,* (p. 252).

35. *Ibid.,* (p. 254).

36. *Ibid.,* (p. 255).

37. *Ibid.,* (p. 268).

38. *Ibid.,* (p. 269).

39. *Ibid.,* (p. 271).

40. Raphael, S. P., (1996). *Jewish Views of the Afterlife.* Northvale:Jason Aronson Incorporated.

41. *Ibid.,* (p. 11-12).

42. *Ibid.,* (p. 16).

43. *Ibid.,* (p. 15).

44. *Ibid.,* (p. 30).

45. *Ibid.,* (p. 14-15).

46. *Ibid.,* (p. 19).

47. *Ibid.,* (p. 21).

48. *Ibid.,* (p. 125).

49. *Ibid.,* (p. 125-127).

50. *Ibid.,* (p. 129).

51. *Ibid.,* (p. 53).

52. *Ibid.,* (p. 55).

53. *Ibid.,* (p. 56).

54. *Ibid.,* (p. 57-58).

55. *Ibid.,* (p. 142-143).

56. *Ibid.,* (p. 144-145).

57. *Ibid.,* (p. 147-148).

58. *Ibid.,* (p. 154).

59. *Ibid.,* (p. 392).

60. Hopfe, L. (1994). *Religions of the World.* (p. 138). Englewood Cliffs: Macmillan College Publishing Company.

61. Van Biema, D. (1997). "Buddhism in America." *Time,* October 13, 1997. (p. 72).

62. Hopfe, L. (1994). *Religions of the World.* (p. 138). Englewood Cliffs: Macmillan College Publishing Company.

63. Eliade, M. (1982). *A History of Religious Ideas: Volume Two: From Gautama Buddha to the Triumph of Christianity.* (p. 72). Chicago: University of Chicago Press.

64. Hopfe, L. (1994). *Religions of the World.* (p. 138). Englewood Cliffs: Macmillan College Publishing Company.

65. *Ibid.,* (p. 138-139).

66. *Ibid.,* (p. 140-141).

67. Eliade, M. (1982). *A History of Religious Ideas: Volume Two: From Gautama Buddha to the Triumph of Christianity.* (p. 93). Chicago: University of Chicago Press.

68. *Ibid.,* (p. 94-95).

69. *Ibid.,* (p. 72).

70. *Ibid.,* (p. 92-93).

71. Sadakata, A. (1997). *Buddhist Cosmology, Philosophy and Origins.* (p. 19). Tokyo: Kosei Publishing Company.

72. *Ibid.,* (p. 25).

73. *Ibid.*

74. *Ibid.,* (p. 26-29).

75. *Ibid.,* (p. 41).

76. *Ibid.,* (p. 42-43).

77. *Ibid.,* (p. 50-51).

78. *Ibid.,* (p. 52-54).

79. *Ibid.,* (p. 55-56).

80. *Ibid.,* (p. 97).

81. *Ibid.,* (p. 69).

82. *Ibid.,* (p. 95-97).

83. *Ibid.,* (p. 99-102).

84. *Ibid.,* (p. 104-105).

85. *Ibid.,* (p. 108).

86. Hopfe, L. (1994). *Religions of the World.* (p. 364). Englewood Cliffs: Macmillan College Publishing Company.

87. *Ibid.*

88. Armstrong, K. (1993). *A History of God.* (p. 132). New York: Ballantine Books.

89. Eliade, M. (1985). *A History of Religious Ideas: Volume Three: From Muhammad to the Age of Reforms.* (p. 62-63). Chicago: The University of Chicago Press.

90. *Ibid.,* (p. 63-64).

91. Hopfe, L. (1994). *Religions of the World.* (p. 369). Englewood Cliffs: Macmillan College Publishing Company.

92. *Ibid.,* (p. 364).

93. *Ibid.,* (p. 366-367).

94. *Ibid.,* (p. 367).

95. *Ibid.,* (p. 367-368).

96. *Ibid.,* (p. 369).

97. *Ibid.*

98. *Ibid.,* (p. 370-371).

99. *Ibid.,* (p. 371).

100. *Ibid.,* (p. 373-375).

101. *Ibid.,* (p. 374-375).

Chapter Four

Eschatology and Historical Events

"One day Henny-Penny was picking up corn in the cornyard when-whack! something hit her on the head. "Goodness gracious me!" said Henny-Penny; "the sky's a-going to fall; I must go and tell the king."[1]

THE SKY IS FALLING

The above excerpt is from a deceptively simple British fairy tale called *Henny-Penny*. In this tale, the character Henny Penny, a chicken, has the notion that the sky is falling - that the world is ending. In a way quite unexpected by Henny, this turns out to be true.

Fairy tales are a sort of myth valued as a medium of entertainment. They are to be differentiated from myths, which often address the serious subject of conducting one's life in harmony with society and nature.[2] Fairy tales have evolved into myths for children. The magic of mythology is that there is a fit for every age of life, because each age has its own truths.[3]

The genesis of fairy tales, or folk tales, may be found in what are euphemistically referred to as "old wives tales," meaning tales with an oral tradition. Since ancient tradition dictated endless hours of mindless, repetitive tasks for women, these steady workers valiantly sought some kind of mental stimulation. As they were spinning wool, women spun stories as well. As with mythology, fairy tales began with an oral tradition, and the stories, once heard, were spread throughout the ancient world. Soldiers, sailors, slaves, merchants, monks, scholars, and crusaders were the verbal traders of these old wives tales.[4] By the fifteenth century, these tales started to enjoy distribution through the revolutionary medium of print.[5]

In the creation of fairy tales, women had to exercise caution. The patriarchal system that dominated many (but not all) cultures was reluctant to acknowledge any erudition that might be forthcoming from women. The formidable power of men, whether found in gov-

Knight, Death and Devil, Albrecht Dürer.

ernmental authority, in religious hierarchy, or in the domination of the husband in the household, had to be respected. So, in the tradition of all historical writers whose content was religious, philosophical, political, or prophetic, women needed to shroud their insights in imagery and metaphor in order to avoid the penalty of one or all of the authorities in the community. In the indirect expression found on the canvas of fairy tales, we can find the insights of women pertaining to the moral dilemmas of their existence.[6]

It is common for all of us to perceive fairy tales as merely a mythological medium for children. Joseph Campbell, in his wonderful *Power Of Myth* written with Bill Moyers[7], tells us that "fairy tales are for children." That is our current cultural understanding of the intended audience for fairy tales. Sources indicate that our contemporary sense of fairy tales being intended for children is a later development. Originally, fairy tales had emotional and moral themes that were more inclined toward an adult audience.[8] Our sense of fairy tales as a children's medium comes from the *editing* of these tales by such notables as Hans-Christian Anderson and the Grimm Brothers.[9]

INTERNAL CRITICAL POINT

In physics, there is a point on the pressure scale that, when attained, *changes, or transforms the state of a substance.*[10] This position is called the *critical point.* After this point, *the substance is no longer the same.* This terminology is applied here because it uniquely describes the intensity of the impact of social and political circumstances on an individual or a group, commensurate with the formation of a millennarian movement. Millennarian movements are the result of events having such a strong impact that *the state of being of a people is transformed. The individual or group is never the same.* Crisis, trauma, and disaster are powerful words, but are insufficient to explain what usually precedes the formation of a millennarian group. Whether a prophet in rapture, a victim of oppression, or a witness to disaster, the attainment of the critical point provides the threshold for entry into a new existence. This is commensurate with rapture.

Internal critical points are as variable as people. It is not uncommon for us to hear or read about a person whose life is completely changed because of one moment of recognition that provided a goal unforeseen and unanticipated. Megan Kanka's mother could not have foreseen her critical moment, when the atrocity committed upon her daughter transformed her life from that of a suburban mother into that of a political activist. Ron Goldman's father never foresaw, and certainly would not have preferred, the life as an author and celebrity that resulted from the murder of his son. How many other lamentable circumstances can we derive? David Koresh at the Waco compound, and Herff Applewhite with the Hale-Bopp suicides are two other painful examples. The World Trade Center bombing in New York City and the Oklahoma City bombing are additional devastations that can generate the critical point of any affected person's existence. How many other less newsworthy events have micro cosmically created critical points in individuals or groups?

There are multitudes of militia and fringe groups extant in contemporary America. Regardless of one's thoughts on the value of such groups, their existence represents in a very real way the attainment of the critical point for a significant number of people. In the fairy-tale that follows, it appears that Henny-Penny, the focus of the tale, has reached her critical point.

A MILLENNARIAN FAIRY TALE

For our purposes, the tale of Henny-Penny is the simplest illustration of some of the crucial attributes of millennarian consciousness. First, let's briefly recount the narrative of this tale. Henny-Penny was going about her usual routine of picking up corn in the cornyard, when suddenly, she is hit on the head by *something* never described in the tale. Was she hit by an object, like an acorn, or was it an intangible idea, dream, or image? The fact that it was a "whack on the head" tells us that it came from *above.* Tradition dictates that divine inspiration comes from above.

Was Henny a prophet? Did she experience rapture? Or was the whack a realization of dissatisfaction with her lot in life, a reaction to the powers that be? This is not an unfamiliar concept. Our discussions of Revelations and Ragnarok include scenarios where both God/gods as well as other characters and things descend from the heavens. Did a tragedy occur in her life? After a powerful tragedy, the world never seems quite the same.

What is important, ultimately, is that Henny *thinks* and *feels* that she has been hit, and that this event is extremely important. This literal and figurative blow to the convention of her life has reconfigured her perception of existence. The comforting constant of the sky above is no more. It is apparently, according to Henny, due to collapse *at any moment.* Times Square was once the regular site of men walking with placards that said "The End Is Near," urgently distributing literature advising readers to prepare for their doom.

This important information, Henny feels, must be reported to the king immediately, and she sets out to do just that. As she proceeds, she encounters several barnyard compatriots: a rooster, a duck, a goose, and a turkey. Each, in their turn, hears her account of her experience and her conviction to see the king. All are persuaded by her fervor over the state of the world, and agree to accompany her on her mission to inform the king. Her vision has become their as well. She has formed a cult. We can relate, identify, and empathize with the devotion of her new followers. We are all familiar with news accounts describing the persuasive power of cults over the impressionable members of our society. Stories such as the situation at Waco and disciples of the Hale-Bopp Comet tell the story of the phenomenal power of a perceived leader-prophet. The participants will *die* for the leader's vision. The same applies to Henny's group. Consumed with her aim, they too will die trying to attain their vision; trying to see the king.

On their way, the barnyard group encounters a fox. They express their burgeoning creed to the fox. The fox listens to their impassioned proselytism, and appears to be persuaded to their mission. He offers them a "shortcut to the king," which is through a narrow and dark hole, the entrance to the cave of the fox. Delighted with this shortened avenue to the king, and a quicker arrival for their declaration of the imminent end of the world, the "sky is falling movement" progresses. All follow the shortcut into the cave, a procession that is led by the newest member of the group, the fox. This shortcut into "a dark and narrow hole" can be seen to parallel "a tunnel," with the members of the group suffering from "tunnel vision;" defined as "an extremely narrow outlook," or "narrow-mindedness."[11] All that this movement cared to see was that they needed to get to the king. So powerful was their need that their instincts about the fox, innate over numerous generations, were ignored for their higher cause.

It is perhaps because of fairy-tales that we have the mythical perception of the clever, sly, deceptive fox, when in reality, a fox is easy hunting. As we continue with Henny's saga, these mythological attributes are in lethal evidence. When Henny's party enters, one by one, into the darkness of the fox's den, he snaps their necks. The last of Henny's companions survives his first blow, and cries out to Henny. Thus Henny runs off home, never to tell the king that the sky is falling.

In the stark simplicity of this tale, we can find some of the attributes of millennarian movements. Henny's experience, whatever it might have been, produced a vision as well as a following. The impact (or whack) of her experience was profound enough, in her vision, to require the attention of the highest governmental authority. Intended or not, Henny became a millennarian leader, and as in contemporary news reports, found disciples who would die for the cause. Let's briefly examine some of the aspects of a millennarian group.

MILLENNARIAN PROFILE

A word commensurate with the history, longevity, continuity, and health for any group is *tradition.* We practice tradition because it comforts us. Regardless of the social, political, or cultural evolutions that are going on around us, in tradition we find the comfort of the familiar. At a determined point in every year, we gather for a purpose. Whether it be for Christmas, Seder, Kwanzaa, or Independence Day, we gather as we always have, in the comfort of each other's company. In these traditions, the world stops at a place where the people are familiar, and we can feel comforted and loved. Tradition need not be practiced annually. Many worship weekly at churches or keep the Sabbath. Tradition can even be observed daily, as with the prayer requirements of Islam.

One of the things that looms as a threat to tradition is change. Seemingly the very antithesis of tradition, change connotes an uneasiness with the absence of the familiar, resulting in uncertainty, doubt, and peril. We have been witness in the late twentieth century to a variety, some might say a plethora, of events that have begun change and social reactionism. These events have included the growth of the AIDS pandemic, the drama of the demise of Communism in Russia, and the horror of genocide in Bosnia and

Rwanda.

History has been peppered with such events, and sadly, genocide is a familiar term. Analogues of the past include the plague of the Black Death, the fall of the Roman Empire, and the massacres during the Crusades. Events of such magnitude have been the agents responsible for social upheaval, which can result in millennarian movements.[12] Millennarian movements are not formed from the mists of the mundane, or the blandness of the ordinary. They occur when the institutions, organizations, or cultural foundations of a society are fundamentally modified, or even destroyed.[13] Eminent events such as invasion, war, or occupation mark the clash of two cultures. The inevitable outcome is that one of the cultures, usually the technologically inferior, suffers the pain and humiliation of defeat and submission. A possible result of this circumstance for the culture forced into servility is called *relative deprivation.*[14]

Relative deprivation represents the difference between what an individual or group *perceives* to be the legitimate expectation of their existence versus the inclination of the dominant culture to satisfy that expectation. The larger the difference between expectation and reality, and the longer the time in which the difference is endured, the larger and deeper the pool of discontent is engendered. What is important is that the displeasure involved only need be a *perception*; reality can be an entirely different matter.[15] Relative deprivation has been experienced by many cultures, sub-cultures, and disenfranchised groups throughout history.

An easy example of relative deprivation can be assigned to the new cult of Christianity of the first century. What this sub-culture desired was the freedom to practice their faith, preach their faith to prospective new members, and live in peace. The dominant culture, that of the Roman Empire, denied this cult the right to live. In reaction to this relative deprivation, John of Patmos wrote *Revelations*.

An alternative form of relative deprivation is *decremental* deprivation[16], which occurs when a group's expectations remain static, but the group's sense of its ability to attain those expectations declines. The most obvious candidates to experience the deprivations described are cults and minority groups.[17] Decremental deprivation can be seen in the large number of fringe and militia groups extant in America today. All of these groups are founded on some expectations that they have been unable to attain for some period of time. Our perception of the character, quality, or sensibility of the demands of these groups is truly irrelevant. In *their* eyes, the expectations they have for their group are totally reasonable. Due process, as well as other systematic redress, has produced no satisfaction for them. Current events already referenced prove in dramatic terms how the extreme frustration experienced by these groups can be manifested. In the deprivation and discontent of the disenfranchised, crushed under the massive weight of oppression that has always been extant in our history, we can find the medium in which many millennarian movements incubate and thrive. And again, it is why the story of the millennium is ever-ending. But groups, like individuals, can react in a variety of ways to tyranny. Some accept their fate passively, while others will exhaust the political avenues available to them in the mainstream of society. But some find their solace in the unconventional route of the creation of a millennarian movement.[18]

Barkun's[19] most interesting work, *Disaster and the Millennium,* informs us of the *inner* forces that may be responsible for steering people toward the visionary extreme of the millennium. One factor is stress, a stimulus that all of us have experienced. But the individual and cultural stress that is operating here is extraordinary. The critical point is attained because the *very existence* of the culture is at stake. The culture must make a simple, yet profound decision: survive or die. If that decision seems obviously bent toward survival, please be reminded that some cultures have chosen to die because it was the only viable option available. The mass suicide at Masada, in the year 73, is a poignant example.

In a revolt against Roman domination that began in the year 66, Jews had captured *Masada,* or *fortress,* a fortified site built on a mountaintop outside of Jerusalem. It had been used as a palace and retreat by King Herod in the previous century. By the year 70, Rome had taken Jerusalem and destroyed the temple. While some Jews took refuge elsewhere, a group called the Zealots, numbering less than one thousand, withdrew to Masada. In a decision to eradicate all resistance, the Roman army sought to retake the fortress. With as many as fifteen thousand troops, the army first built a wall to prevent escape by the Zealots, and then built a ramp up the mountain to attack. In 73, with their capture in sight, the Zealots chose to die by their own hand rather than be taken and massacred by the

Romans.

Even having chosen survival, at least temporarily, a culture still reels from the enormous toll of oppression. One way that this is demonstrated is by the self- destructive behavior of the culture's members. The history of alcohol and substance abuse[20] endured by Native Americans and the neglected impoverished in urban areas of this country are a powerful illustration of this point. The effect of oppression can also be observed in contemporary Russia, a country staggering from the vacuum created by the vaporization of Communism. The transition to capitalism has rewarded a few, but most have been left out of the new influx of wealth. For these unfortunates, alcohol and nicotine addition has continued unabated. Hospitals and sanitariums are filled with patients under the age of fifty, who have directed themselves towards death in numbers unparalleled in the rest of the world. Sadly, the burden of subjugation can cause a culture or sub-culture to choose to die overnight as in Masada, or slowly and tortuously as in modern day Russia.

Survival for a culture extraordinarily stressed by unanticipated change lies in its ability to alleviate the enormous pressure placed upon it. One way to assuage this formidable influence is to recreate the principles that formulate the existence of the culture. In the presence of circumstances that nullify those principles, a new scenario is required, platformed with new axioms attuned to the difficult circumstances at hand.[21] In this recreation, we see a microcosm of the cyclical cosmogony of the universe already described. For the oppressed culture, its fundamental precepts and order have been crushed into the chaos of stress and impending doom. Creation, or more accurately, recreation, is required to bring chaos into a new order. For the culture or sub-culture that chooses to survive, this is called *revitalization*.[22] With revitalization, we revert to our past, to the time when myths were created and the answers to the "ineffable mysteries"[23] were sought. The services of a prophet or seer are again required to derive meaning from a new set of unexplained occurrences. The skill with which the seer produces a persuasive vision capable of alleviating the angst of the people is important. Revelations that sway a few are acknowledged as cults, while those that move many become religious or political movements.[24]

Over more than a half-century, at a cost of *trillions* of rubles, the Communist military machine of the Soviet Union sought global superiority. This country engaged in an enormously expensive political, military, nuclear, and space competition with the United States. In its efforts to win this competition, the needs of its people were ignored, and their sense of relative and decremental deprivation became maximized. By 1991, the Soviet economy had collapsed, and a new order was demanded by the previously disenfranchised. Under Gorbachev, a new program called *perestroika*–restructuring–became the Soviet revitalization.

Barkun's review of theorists and theories includes the concept of the *true society*.[25] The true society is the world in which an individual, or a culture, maintains a sense of identification. The concept describes, in degrees of intensity, what is important to an individual or group. The true society is usually strongest at the core family level, followed by extended family, then religious community, nationality, and so on. At each successive extension, the true society becomes weaker.[26] For example, a pebble is dropped into a pond. At impact, a rise in the water is observed. This ring of water is the true society at its most powerful, commensurate with the mother-child relationship. The ring then dissipates into a ripple, and as it progresses away from the epicenter, it grows more and more faint until it disappears. The true society is that part of the world of the individual or group that cannot be compromised. The destruction of the true society is simply but inexorably a *critical point* for the unfortunate victims. There are no societal explanations or entreaties that can possibly assuage the anguish of an assault on the true society.[27]

A recent and profoundly tragic example of the impact of the assault and destruction of the true society was the Oklahoma City bombing. The building that was destroyed contained Federal offices as well as a day care center, so it housed citizens of all ages. The victims, from pre-school children to senior citizens, were representatives of the epicenter of the true society for many people. One man's pregnant wife was killed, and the essence of his true society destroyed. At the trial connected with this tragedy, the man related that his life was *transformed, not the same.* His bout with depression and alcohol produces nothing but compassion. This tragedy has, unfortunately, produced the "functional analogue of mental illness,"[28] because in the absence of our true society, our critical point is attained and we are, for at least a period, not the same as before.

Disaster deprives the individual, and groups, of the comfort and blessings of the ordinary. Familiarity is a situation labeled as mundane and predictable. In its absence, however, a longing for its succor is generated. The familiarities with their confining rules, once considered disposable, are now deemed precious, but have been replaced by abnormality. A new comfort must be sought that articulates a new reality.[29] Some historical examples of such a perspective follow.

REVELATIONS & EARLY CHRISTIAN HISTORY

John of Patmos painted a picture of the end of the world that was a relief to the early Christians. If the world ended, their horrible oppression at the hands of Rome would end, and they needed to feel that their salvation was close at hand.[30] What made the apocalypse attractive was that it was laden with two types of rewards. The spiritual salvation of the faithful was promised, but there was also a perceived materialistic aspect to the millennium. The Christian cultists anticipated rewards commensurate with those that were being enjoyed by the conquering Romans. Needless to say, the appeal of material compensation for their pain and suffering was a powerful draw for this fledgling group. John's vision would hold the Christian community in its grip for two hundred-fifty years. For much of that period, the millennium was anticipated and ardently desired.[31] But it never happened, and as the years passed, the dream faded.

In the time required for the dissipation of that fantasy, history took a few interesting turns. Early in the fourth century, Rome proclaimed a new emperor, who would become known to history as Constantine the Great. On the eve of a major battle in the year 312, Constantine dreamed that Christ directed him to inscribe all of the soldiers' shields with the first two letters of his name. In a second vision the next day, Constantine is reputed to have seen a cross over the sun, as well as the words "in this sign you will be the victor."[32] Constantine was victorious in battle and perceived Christ as responsible. The Christian persecution was thus ended. The Edict of Milan, enacted in 313, decreed that the goodwill of the Roman Empire would be extended to Christians.[33] The terror that spawned the avenging vision of Revelations was gone.

The whole concept of the millennium started to suffer from disfavor for other reasons as well. The cult that immersed itself in the millennium promise was no longer a cult, but an official religion. There were no more martyred to grieve, no more persecuted to comfort, no more rapturous propaganda of a New Jerusalem required.[34] With this simple declaration of the legality of Christianity, Constantine may have made one of the most critical decisions ever.[35] By ensuring the survival of Christianity, and providing the powerful medium of encouragement, Constantine literally changed the course of history. You are now invited to re-examine how much of the principal events of history, both the shining and the tarnished, were the product of the spiritual, political, and social power of Christianity, a small cult nourished into a dominating force.

AUGUSTINE

St. Augustine (354-430), who was Bishop of Hippo (in what is now Algeria), provided a new view of Revelations, and therefore the millennium. Augustine is regarded as one of the most influential spokespersons of Christian thought; someone who's perspective remained unquestioned for a thousand years.[36] An important part of understanding the passion of Augustine's views requires a perspective on who Augustine was. According to history, it appears that Augustine was not always a saint.[37] But regardless of weaknesses, which we all have in abundance, Augustine was a keenly intelligent, gifted person who spent many years searching for a truth that would yield a definite meaning to his existence. He examined many philosophies in his search, as well as himself. In the year 386, Augustine is reputed to have had a revelation in which a child's voice told him to read the Scriptures, an experience that led him to Christianity.[38] Augustine attained his spiritual and philosophical being through the vicissitudes of human experience, which was enhanced by intellect, and graced by a bonafide leap of faith.[39] This perspective would serve to define the temper of Augustine's writings, which are the chronicles of his thoughts and espousals forged by a conviction that religion was an individual, internal, and entirely spiritual experience.[40]

One of Augustine's most renowned works is *The City of God*, a treatise of tremendous importance on the Christian view of history, from his eloquent perspective. The title of the work refers to the eternal life or residence in heaven that should be the aspiration of each *individual*, and which is attainable only through the Church.[41] The concepts of this view dictated the Christian view of the millennium for centuries. When Augustine points the attention of the *City of God* toward Revelations, his view is very consistent with the attributes of his personal struggle toward his own spiritual niche.

One concern that Augustine retained regarding Revelations was the seeming promise of material gain for those found in God's favor and destined for the New Jerusalem. This heavenly city had been interestingly equipped, as the biblical text indicates, with some very earthly accoutrements; gates made from sapphire and walls laden with precious stones.[42] Images such as these were part of the powerful lure that Revelations held for the painfully deprived members of the Christian cult, since they believed in its verbatim veracity.

The chronicle of Revelations, as we have seen, was understood by its early readers to be an epic played on the canvas of the very universe: heaven, earth, and hell. On this enormous scale, Revelations depicted a phenomenon that seemed to be clearly external to its audience, with the reader as a witness of the ultimate happening. Augustine's perspective put an end to literal interpretation. The *literal* interpretation of Revelations, as well as other Scriptures that seemed to defy realistic consideration, conflicted with the spiritual inclinations of Augustine. He therefore sought a new approach, one that would modify the meaning of the more extraordinary and fantastic passages of the Scriptures.[43] This would serve to combat any misunderstandings of the rewards offered at the culmination of the events of Revelations.

The fifth century produced a new narrative form called *allegory.* This new medium of form and presentation provided an official avenue of expression that communicated a symbolic meaning intended to be more important than its literal meaning.[44] In Augustine's time, the events that dictated his vision and directed his writing were as important as those of John of Patmos. He seized upon the allegorical construct to transform the material aspects of the *Book of Revelations*, as well as other Scriptures, for reasons that were theologically as well as historically relevant. The era of the writing of *The City of God* (413-426) finds Augustine, along with many others, looking over their shoulders at the political events of the day. The blunt persecution of the followers of John of Patmos and their desire for the destruction of the Roman Empire had been replaced by the concern that the Empire *would* be destroyed by the Visigoths or some other savage horde. The Empire, once the enemy, was now the protector. The times had certainly changed, and the message of Revelations changed correspondingly.

In the same way that we consider our own experiences in whatever we undertake in our lives, Augustine brought his circumstances to his writings. Revelations, according to Augustine, was not an awesome display of good and evil acted out on the stage of the cosmos, which is the interpretation fancied by the earlier members of the Christian cult. Instead, it was an allegorical presentation of the *individual and internal* struggles of all.[45]

An interesting illustration of the internal predisposition of Christianity, and therefore of Augustine, can be found in the architecture and design of contemporaneous places of worship. Pagan temples of the era were noted for the elaborate decoration and presentation of their *exterior* edifices. Their interiors have been noted to be bare. The gods were apparently beings that acted out their dramas somewhere *out there*.[46] This pagan perception is not unfamiliar. Aren't we all parties to the current media preoccupation with celebrities? We are all witness, whether by effort or exposure, to the details of the lives of people who have made the critical decision to pursue or accept fame. They have become, in a sense, demi-gods. Externally, these gods are beautiful, and for some, worthy of admiration. Internally and meaningfully, however, they provide us with merely a distraction or an observation. They are admired for what some of us, mere everyday people, would like to be. Observed on the screen or in photographs, these players often exhibit qualities and attributes that we cast upon them, because we would love to see those same facets in ourselves. That psychological process is called projection. Isn't it interesting that the machine allowing movies to be viewed onscreen is called a *projector*?

Early Christian churches, on the other hand, were designed in a completely opposite fashion. The aim was to draw the faithful and prospective faithful *within,* into the beauty of an existence that was somehow removed from the familiar world.[47] The architectural message is that the kingdom of Christ is removed from this world.[48] To this day, a visit to a major cathedral will provide a similar experience. Although the exteriors have become more elaborate over the centuries, the interiors of churches and cathedrals are still an attraction.

Upon entering these truly special places, doors close behind the visitor, and the world goes away. There is no more traffic, noise, or pollution. However, there are stained glass windows, pillars, vaults, high ceilings, and an *otherworldly ambiance*. The 1997 visitor, without much effort, can imagine him/herself to be in the same place as an 1897, or 1797 visitor. In the church or cathedral, entry into the sacred space represented the extraction of the being from the madness of the profane world, and an entry into the sacred world. Time *stops*. The internal, spiritual world takes its proper place where there is no time, and the present, the sought encounter with God, is both momentary and everlasting. During this interlude, there is no profane world, only a moment sought for peace of mind or soul.

CHARLEMAGNE

Norman Cohn's *The Pursuit of the Millennium*[49] is rightfully considered a seminal text in research on the end of days, because of its detail in depicting the mindset of the people of the Middle Ages. Included in his work is a presentation of the importance of Charlemagne's reign, from the perspectives of his impact both prior to and following his death. History records Charlemagne as one of the most powerful men in history, for in his time, Europe knew no higher earthly authority. His kingdom included what is now France, Germany, Belgium, Holland, Switzerland, a notable part of Italy, and a small section of Spain.[50] It did not take scholars of Charlemagne's era very long to make the connection between his influence and that of the renowned Roman Emperors of the past.[51]

In the winter of the year 800, Charlemagne went to Rome to come to the aid of Pope Leo III. Leo had been experiencing difficulties of a political nature with the local nobility. Charlemagne successfully settled the dispute, and remained in Rome for Christmas.[52]

On Christmas Day, 800, Charlemagne attended Mass at St. Peter's Basilica. When he arose from prayer, Pope Leo crowned him Holy Roman Emperor. At that moment, Charlemagne had become a figure of unqualified power and stature, taking the step from man into legend.

For some time, Cohn states, the peasants saw themselves as participants in the final events that would culminate in the millennium. They studiously attended to the perceived signs that were the harbingers of the final days.[53] Among the indicators that the peasants anticipated were that of "the great emperor," who in the last days

Fourth Horseman of the Apocalypse, Jean Colombe

would find his way to Jerusalem.[54] Ancient prophecies originally called for the last emperor to rule from Constantinople, but subsequent translations resulted in different conclusions.[55] The spectacle of Charlemagne's coronation allowed observers of the time to imagine that the Last Emperor might come from the west.[56]

Charlemagne died in 814, but legends are never far from those who revere them. Near the end of the eleventh century, the notion of a Crusade was gathering support. As the excitement around such an event continued, it began to circulate among the peasantry that Charlemagne would rise from the dead to lead the Crusade.[57] Others believed that Charlemagne had never really died at all, but had simply been sleeping until the hour of his return, to conquer and inaugurate the age that was to precede the end of days.[58]

THE YEAR 1000

The idea of a particular cycle attaining its conclusion, then being followed by a succeeding cycle, is part of the folklore and mythology of many cultures.[59] The vision of *Revelations* had taken root in the consciousness of many Europeans during the first millennium. In his writings, John of Patmos had been very clear about the significance of a thousand-year period.[60] As the end of the first millennium drew to a close, its Biblical import was not lost on many. But details about this era, in terms of historical documentation, are somewhat disappointing.

What is available does give some insight into the lifestyle and mindset of the times. Religion and the Church were an important part of the existence of the era. However little the devoted may have understood about their faith, their allegiance was unqualified.[61] As the tenth century progressed towards its inevitable close, the deceit and shame that was generated by the Papacy did not tarnish the luster of belief. The leap of faith had been taken, and the coming of God and His Kingdom were accepted as fact.[62] Life was not at all easy; it was a passage of hard work, minimal rewards, and shadows cast by the omnipresent specters of affliction and hunger. The focus of life's activities was the Church: attending Mass and prayer meetings with monks, maintaining the Church's properties, and delivering the first of one's harvest to the parish.[63]

The sense that time was winding down became widespread, and the idea that a cycle was concluding was accepted.[64] For a peasantry that had experienced little of the joy of life, there was a feeling of anticipation that something better was not far off. The time to the millennium grew shorter, and as rumors of the presence of the devil abounded, the weather and the heavens were examined for signs of the end of days. Penance and penitence were practiced with increasing fervor, the saints and their relics were beseeched, and pilgrimages to Jerusalem and Rome were undertaken.[65]

But at the appointed time, nothing happened. It was thought that the date of the birth of Christ had been miscalculated, but as time continued to pass, there was the sense that the world was not going to end after all.[66] By the millennium of the Crucifixion in 1033, it was felt that the penance, the vows, and the pilgrimages had accomplished the task of averting the millennium.[67]

THE FIRST CRUSADE

One of the most elaborate images of *Revelations* is that of the New Jerusalem, the heavenly city. The spiritual promise of this city was perhaps surpassed by the material or worldly imagery employed by its writer.

"The wall was built of diamond, the city of pure gold, like clear glass. The foundations of the wall were faced with all kinds of precious stones: the first with diamond, the second lapis lazuli, the third turquoise, the fourth crystal, the fifth agate, the sixth ruby, the seventh gold quartz, the eighth malachite, the ninth topaz, the tenth emerald, the eleventh sapphire, and the twelfth amethyst. The twelve gates were twelve pearls, each gate being made of a single pearl, and the main street of the city was pure gold, transparent as glass."[50]

What is often lost in the revisiting of history are the subtleties of *perspective* and *sensation*. Only the contemporaries of the event can accurately feel these experiences of being. For example, younger viewers of the Zapruder film depicting the Kennedy Assassination are witness to the tragic murder of a man that they know was President of the United States. Those of us with a memory of that time recognize that there was much more involved than the death of a man who happened to be President. Kennedy, who became President at the age of forty-three, represented the prominence of a country that was young, with power and wealth that seemed limitless. Our memories tell us that issues long ignored, such as the discrimination against African-Americans, were to be addressed by this young man. The disabled, and the exclusionary issues that they faced, were also to be addressed by this President, who had a mentally retarded sister. The sheer confidence of this man, as well as his nation, was illustrated in his unheard-of promise *to put a man on the moon!* This leader was in his prime, as was the nation. This was Camelot, glowing in the ideal, free of the tarnish that would later cloud the Kennedy legacy. Some observers have declared that the United States has been in decline for some time. If that is so, a suggested time for the commencement of this decline might be November 1963.

The point here is that a time, an era, or an age has an essence that is completely meaningful only to the inhabitants of that time. In the recording, whether by pen, print, or visual image, *something is lost,* and that is the actual climate of the times, available only to the era's inhabitants.

In much the same way, it is hard for us to understand the power and the aura of *Jerusalem* to eleventh century peasants. The importance of this city is very much a part of the tradition of several religious orientations (Nirvana, Xanadu, Valhalla, Heaven), but *Revelations* made it a magical place. For eleventh century men, Jerusalem was a place of "glittering and magical splendour,"[51] whose import and promise is lost to us. The word *Jerusalem,* when spoken, engendered "psychological reactions and conjured up particular eschatological notions."[52] Jerusalem was the location of Christ's passion and triumphant resurrection. It was also the location of the spectacular city described in *Revelations.* Jerusalem was the ultimate Christian meeting place, the goal of all pilgrimages, and the place at the end of days to which the faithful will gather; the city of the righteous, the city of paradise.[53]

Toward the end of the eleventh century, the concern of the papacy with the safety and sanctity of the Eastern Church reached its peak. In the year 1095, at a council in Clermont, France, Pope Urban II called for the end of the "desecration of the holy places,"[54] with Jerusalem being the holiest of all. Urban called for volunteers to embark for Jerusalem on this holy mission, with the promise that all prior sins would be absolved. The response was overwhelming. Urban illustrated an appalling picture of the activities of Muslims and the menace presented by the Turks. Cleverly, he had followed the tradition of other Popes in assigning the survival of the entire Church to the emancipation of one of its small clusters.[55]

The call for the Crusade was made and the protection of Jerusalem, the holiest of cities, was demanded. Hordes of the peasantry heeded the call and set out to free the holy city of Jerusalem, the city of the millennium.

The word *Crusade* comes from the latin *crux*, meaning cross, and Urban's call was seen as the injunction in Matthew: *"Anyone who does not take up his cross and follow in my footsteps is not worthy of me. Anyone who finds his life will lose it; anyone who loses his life for my sake will find it."*[56] Armed with these words and a symbol of the cross, the peasantry went off by the thousands to Jerusalem. All were familiar with the heavenly image of Jerusalem described above, and many of the uneducated peasants actually thought they were going to the magical city paved with gold.[57] They were hoping for a share of the material plenty that appeared to be waiting for God's faithful. These unfortunates were desperately poor, and successive years of crop failures made their already miserable lives even more arduous. For them this eschatological trek left little to lose, and in their fantasies, everything to gain. The Pope himself, when he called for the Crusade, spoke of the possibility of "laying up treasures on earth as well as in heaven," and "the remission of your sins with the assurance of the imperishable glory of the kingdom of heaven."[58]

In the spring of 1096, the first wave of Crusaders set out on their mission. Urban's call was made in France, but word spread, and the faithful from England, Scotland, Spain, Germany, and Italy also responded. The Crusaders were to travel through Germany and the Balkans and gather in Constantinople[59], but there were to be some unanticipated events during the march.

In the gathering of the Crusaders, we are witness to the power of religion over its believers. Upon Urban's call, thousands put their lives on hold, and prepared to do as commanded: "Deus Vult!"- God wills it! But something more discomforting, even terrifying comes to the fore. In this Crusade, we are witness to the horror of religious frenzy.[60] When news of the Crusade spread, it was disseminated with fervor and conviction by the preachers of the day, especially a monk known as Peter the Hermit. His gifted speaking abilities and power of persuasion emptied entire towns of its men, women, and children in order to join him on his Crusade, which was dubbed the People's Crusade.[61] The prospect of material and spiritual reward for carrying out God's will to slaughter the Muslims created a hysteria that could not be controlled. As Peter and his followers wandered through Germany delirious with passion for their heavenly mission, they slaughtered many thousands of Jews, the only perceived infidels who happened to be available at the time.[62] However, their frenzy was no match for the Turkish army, and many Crusaders were killed in Asia Minor.[64]

In June of 1099, the goal of the Crusade was accomplished: Jerusalem was "liberated." The heavenly city was plundered and despoiled by the Crusaders themselves, those assigned to protect and cherish it. The Crusade was now over. Jerusalem was in ruins and the millennium, once again, did not occur. For most of those who had survived the conflagration, it was time to go home.

THE BLACK DEATH

We have already suggested that disaster can be the source of millennarian thinking. One of the most notable disasters in the entire history of the world was the bubonic plague, or The Black Death, which struck much of the known world in the fourteenth century. This horrible affliction began in the Gobi desert in the first quarter of the fourteenth century. Over the next eighty years, it took the lives of 45 million Chinese. The arrival of the year 1349 found a full

Burning of Infected Clothes During the Black Plague, manuscript detail.

third of the Muslim world wiped out. At the same time, The Black Death had arrived in Europe, where it would claim 25 million victims. Ultimately, a third of the population of *the entire world* was wiped out.[65]

The Black Death was caused by a bacterium that was communicated to humans by lice and rats already infected. Most frequently, the victim was afflicted by chills, fever, fatigue, and swollen lymph nodes. The plague's name came from the victim's hemorrages, which turned black.[66] In addition to the bubonic plague, the Black Death could also take the form of pneunomic plague, a respiratory disease, and septicemic plague, a disease of the blood. The victims of pneumatic plague are ridden with a fever that turns the complexion a dark rose color. Sneezing fits, coughing, and the appearance of bloody sputum in the terminal stages follow.[67] The sequence of symptoms in this plague is recorded to this day in this childhood song:

Ring around the rosy
Pocket full of posy
Achoo, Achoo
We all fall down.

The *ring* in the song refers to a circular folk dance. The *rosy* refers to the color a plague victim's complexion becomes. The *posy* refers to scented material which was carried in an attempt to mask the stench of the dead, who were so numerous that neither graves nor bonfires could be constructed fast enough to accommodate them. *Achoo, achoo* (sometimes *Ashes, ashes*) approximates the sounds of the victim in a fit of sneezing. *We all fall down* is the sad but realistic anticipation of falling down dead.[68]

In fourteenth century Europe, the scourge of the plague was just the latest and most severe of the cosmic tribulations that many assumed must have been sent by God. Comets, solar eclipses, and floods had all been witnessed and reported.[69] Surely, it was felt, these must be the signs described in Revelations. More frightening still was the fact that no one could explain the plague's causes or the sometimes unusual manifestations it had. For example, some towns were virtually wiped out, while others remained unharmed.[70] We

The Triumph of Death, Fresco detail by Francesco Traini,
Camposanto, Pisa, c. 1350.

can only approximate the devastating impact of this plague by gauging our own horror at the threat of the AIDS pandemic in the 1980's when there was no sign of an effective treatment.

The Black Death had an impact even for survivors. Firstly, there was an overwhelming preoccupation with death, which was literally all around. This fixation is illustrated in the art of the era, which displays an obsession with the phases of decay experienced by a corpse after death.[71] Secondly, this horror inspired a renewed religious fervor, with the hope that God might forgive their sins, which must be great indeed if they generated signs of the end of the world. This rejuvenated pursuit of religion took at least one odd turn in the form of the flagellants. These groups, sometimes numbering in the thousands, would arrive in a town and head for the church or cathedral. Once there, they called out to God for forgiveness, and then these penitents proceeded to flagellate themselves with such force that their bodies were rendered swollen and bruised.[72]

Their pleadings were apparently not heard. The plague would repeatedly return during the rest of the century. The following excerpts from an historical account communicate the lamentable and insidious wrath of the plague:

"*Then the grievous plague penetrated the seacoasts from Southampton and came to Bristol and there almost the whole strength of the town had died, struck as it were by sudden death...And there were small prices for everything on account of the fear of death. For there were very few who cared about riches or anything else...Sheep and cattle went wandering over fields and through crops and there was no one to go and drive and gather them...The Scots, hearing of the cruel pestilence of the English, believed it had come to them from the avenging hand of God...After the pestilence, many buildings, great and small, fell into ruins in every city...for lack of inhabitants, likewise many villages and hamlets became desolate, not a house being left in them, all having died who dwelt there; and it was probable that many such villages would never be inhabited.*"[91]

The population of Europe did not start to increase until the middle of the fifteenth century.[92]

COLUMBUS

The opening years of the fifteenth century mark the commencement of a period of almost two hundred years of cultural and scientific advances. The world seemed to awaken with a creative fervor after the relative grogginess of the earlier Middle Ages. This awakening can be illustrated by the invention of the printing press, as well as the movement resulting in the Protestant Reformation. The complete list of events occurring during this period would be quite extensive. The power of the Church during this era required these accomplishments to be viewed through a religious prism.[93] Particular attention was paid to another notable and familiar example of the achievements of this period: the voyage of Columbus.

One can understand that the implications of the discovery of Columbus on the fifteenth century European world must have been tremendous. Had our current media been present at that time, the coverage would have been awesome. Contemporary parallels might include the landing on the moon in 1969, or the recent Pathfinder mission to Mars. Events of this caliber have the power to make the world stop, if even for a moment, to take notice, and assign significance to the occurrence.

Theologically, the discovery of America raised difficult issues.[94]

For the contemporaries of Columbus, the New World might just as well have been a new planet. This was, clearly, a threat to the understanding of the order of the world of the time. In the opinion of Christopher Columbus, the discovery was nothing less than an eschatological event, one in which the influence of God was active in the formation of a "miracle." For Columbus, this was not simply a voyage to new lands or a new world. It was, he felt, the journey of a man (himself), chosen by God to find the *new heaven* and *new earth* that John espoused in *Revelations.*[95]

What is revisited in the chronicle of Columbus' journey, and will be documented further in the chronology of the period, is the sense that the decrepitude of the world would lead to its end, and its subsequent renewal. To an eschatologically minded man, as Columbus apparently was, the pristine world of the West Indies must have appeared as Paradise Regained. The power of this discovery could not be underestimated. All practitioners of Christian, Muslim, or Judaic religion, to this day, have been taught to bemoan the actions of our mutual parents, Adam and Eve, for being cast from Paradise, a lost place. Perhaps Columbus felt that he had found it. The scars of civilization must have seemed particularly ugly by contrast.

The eschatological mindset of Columbus did not end with his heralded, yet disputed, discovery. Columbus calculated that the end of the world would befall mankind 155 years after his voyage. Any disappointment over the failure of that prediction was seemingly tempered by the influx of gold from the "new heaven and new earth," that would regain Jerusalem from the infidel.[96]

THE REFORMATION

Previously we have mentioned the pivotal historical impact of Constantine's decision to provide the legal medium for the proliferation of Christianity. If there is a match to the historical significance of this event, a good place to look might be the Protestant Reformation.

The era in which the reformation took place was, as we have said, one of renewed accomplishment. While that might seem to be the backdrop to an era of contentment and good feeling, this was not the case. There was a sense of malaise that was related to a variety of factors. During this time, Europe was just beginning to recover from the wrath of the plague, a perceived sign of the tremendous dissatisfaction of God with mankind. This helped to feed the already established sense that the world had grown old, that it was, apparently, time for the final age predicted by *Revelations*.[97] What also added to the pessimism of the day was the individual and collective struggle of the people with their relationship between God and the Church. If this seems odd to our contemporary sensibilities, it is because we find it difficult to grasp the sheer power and influence of the Church over the daily lives of these people. The passage of time had allowed the faithful to witness and hear examples of the abuse of that apparent omnipotence. Massacres in God's name and the sale of indulgences, which literally allowed the rich to buy their way into heaven, were among the offences. The sixteenth century would bring with it a new atrocity: witch hunting. This would claim the lives of thousands more over the next two centuries, in Europe and America.[98] The witch trials were replete with the maximally lurid depictions of orgies with Satan. This tragedy represents a "collective fantasy" of the highest order, and sadly, a reaction against "a repressive religion and an apparently inexorable God." God had become a being to be feared and placated.[99]

This point is poignantly illustrated by Martin Luther, the person most easily identified with the Reformation. His writings lament his helplessness before God. Regardless of his extraordinary efforts to live a spiritual existence, he felt he had, and always would, come up short in God's measure. The God of Martin Luther was a God of fury.[100] Luther's frustration needed a target. While God was so painfully elusive, His instrument, the Church, was totally accessible. And while the perception that the world had grown old had already been stated, a new, revolutionary declaration was that the *Church* had grown old.[101] A millennium had passed since Augustine had assigned *Revelations* to allegory, although its literal presentation was always popular with the peasantry. But the timbre of the era of the late fifteenth and early sixteenth centuries found writers and observers looking more and more to *Revelations* to make sense of the events surrounding them.[102]

Luther himself had a series of writings about *Revelations*. In his writing, in 1522, he is apparently astounded by the symbolism of *Revelations*, admitting that some of the book escapes him.[103] In 1545, Luther sees *Revelations* in a different light. His writing distinguishes between express prophecy, or literal foretelling; symbolic prophecy, which includes interpretations; and finally, symbolic prophecy, or without interpretation. *Revelations* is clearly the final category. Luther concludes that its symbolism will be apparent at the appropriate time[104], which meant the present.

The angst within the Church-dominated society of Luther cannot be overstated. We have already discussed *rapture, the critical point,* and *the true society.* These pivotal terms describe the circumstances that require the establishment of a set of new ideas in order to make existence meaningful. In much the same way that the early Christians felt smothered by the power and influence of Rome, the reformers of Luther's day felt enclosed by the Church. John of Patmos, or whoever the writer(s) of *Revelations* might have been, had reached across a millennium to convince a new set of believers that justice was at hand.[105]

Luther was the first to provide us with a practical method for dealing with the complexity of the symbolism of *Revelations. Revelations*, for Luther and other concerned observers to follow, became a blueprint, one followed to this day.[106] Luther's logic regarding Revelations was that it was indecipherable because it was prophetic, describing events that had not happened at the time of its writing. However, as events transpired, they could be compared to the images depicted in the text, searching for a match.[107] And in Luther's eyes, the number of circumstances corresponding with the images of *Revelations* was disconcertingly large.

The oppressive Rome of *Revelations*, as we have said, was replaced by the tryannical Church. The realization that the Pope was the Anti-Christ[108], was not only an easy association, it was not even original. This was not the first era to draw that conclusion, nor would it be the last. But as he searched *Revelations* for other correlations, Luther did not come up empty-handed. Where *Revelations* depicted the arrival of evil angels, Luther translated this as the presence of heretics.[109] The destruction of Babylon is the destruction of the papacy. The millennium in which Satan was to be bound, Luther determined, *had already passed*, having begun with the writing of *Revelations*. Therefore, Luther deduced, the last days were *now*.[110]

Anyone can predict the end of the world, and certainly many people have, as we will discover in a later chapter. Luther's sense of the end of days is important, however, because of who he was. Luther was a multilingual scholar of the highest caliber, committed and devoted to arriving at a meaningful understanding with his God. He had risked his life, and his soul, to discover why the Church, in its absolute power, failed.[111] These credentials made his eschatological thought important for his contemporaries. Whether Lutheran, Calvinist, or Anglican, many suscribed to the important apocalyptic impression left by the era.[112] Its power was such that it permeated European thinking, and moreover would find its way, in the years following, to the New World.

Chapter Four Bibliography

1. Arbuthnot, M.H. (1952) *Time for Fairy Tales Old and New.* (p. 12) New York: Scott, Foresman.
2. Campbell, J.,with Moyers B. (1988) *The Power of Myth.* (p. 138) New York: Doubleday Press.
3. Ibid.
4. Arbuthnot, M.H. (1952) *Time for Fairy Tales Old and New.* (p. 4) New York: Scott, Foresman.
5. *Ibid.*
6. *Fairy Tales/Internet*
7. Campbell, J.,with Moyers B. (1988) *The Power of Myth.* (p. 138) New York: Doubleday Press.
8. Arbuthnot, M.H. (1952) *Time for Fairy Tales Old and New.* (p. 3) New York: Scott, Foresman.
9. *Fairy Tales/Internet*
10. *Microsoft Encarta Encyclopedia.* (1996). Critical point.
11. *Microsoft Encarta Dictionary.* (1996). Tunnel vision.
12. Barkun, M. (1986) *Disaster and the Millennium.* (p. 45) Syracuse: Syracuse University Press.
13. *Ibid.*
14. *Ibid.,* (p.34).
15. *Ibid.*
16. *Ibid.*
17. *Ibid.*
18. *Ibid.,* (p.37).
19. Barkun, M. (1986) *Disaster and the Millennium.* Syracuse: Syracuse University Press.
20. *Ibid.,* (p. 38-39).
21. *Ibid.,* (p. 39).
22. *Ibid.*
23. Campbell, J. (1969).*Primitive Mythology.* (p. 54) New York: Penguin Books.
24. Barkun, M. (1986) *Disaster and the Millennium.* (p. 39). Syracuse: Syracuse University Press.

25. *Ibid.,* (p. 50).

26. *Ibid.,* (p. 51).

27. *Ibid.*

28. *Ibid.,* (p.56).

29. *Ibid.*

30. Tuveson, E.L. (1972). *Millennium and Utopia.* (p. 9). Gloucester: Peter Smith.

31. *Ibid.,* (p. 11).

32. *Microsoft Encarta Encyclopedia.* (1996) Constantine the Great.

33. *Ibid.*

34. Tuveson, E.L. (1972). *Millennium and Utopia.* (p. 14). Gloucester: Peter Smith.

35. Claster, J.N., (1982). *The Medieval Experience: 300-1400.* (p. 35) New York: New York University Press.

36. *Ibid.,* (p. 47).

37. *Ibid.*

38. *Ibid.,* (p. 48).

39. *Ibid.*

40. Tuveson, E.L. (1972). *Millennium and Utopia.* (p. 16). Gloucester: Peter Smith.

41. Claster, J.N., (1982). *The Medieval Experience: 300-1400.* (p. 49). New York: New York University Press.

42. Mayer, H.E., (1988). *The Crusades.* (p. 11). Oxford: Oxford University Press.

43. Tuveson, E.L. (1972). *Millennium and Utopia.* (p. 16). Gloucester: Peter Smith.

44. *Microsoft Encarta Encyclopedia.* (1996). Augustine.

45. Tuveson, E.L. (1972). *Millennium and Utopia.* (p. 17). Gloucester: Peter Smith.

46. Claster, J.N., (1982). *The Medieval Experience: 300-1400.* (p. 25). New York: New York University Press.

47. *Ibid.*

48. *Ibid.*

49. Cohn, N. (1970). *The Pursuit of the Millennium.* New York: Oxford University Press.

50. Claster, J.N., (1982). *The Medieval Experience: 300-1400.* (p. 119). New York: New York University Press.

51. *Ibid.,* (p. 120).

52. *Ibid.,* (p. 121).

53. Cohn, N. (1970). *The Pursuit of the Millennium.* (p. 71). New York: Oxford University Press.

54. *Ibid.*

55. *Ibid.*

56. *Ibid.*

57. *Ibid.,* (p. 72).

58. *Ibid.*

59. Strozier, C.B. (1994). *Apocalypse: on the Psychology of Fundamentalism in America.* (p.155). Boston: Beacon Press.

60. *Ibid.*

61. Claster, J.N., (1982). *The Medieval Experience: 300-1400.* (p. 164). New York: New York University Press.

62. *Ibid.*

63. *Ibid.*

64. Strozier, C.B. (1994). *Apocalypse: on the Psychology of Fundamentalism in America.* (p.156). Boston: Beacon Press.

65. Eliade, M. (1985). *A History of Religious Ideas, Volume 3: From Muhammad to the Age of Reforms.* (p. 88). Chicago: The University of Chicago Press.

66. Strozier, C.B. (1994). *Apocalypse: on the Psychology of Fundamentalism in America.* (p.156). Boston: Beacon Press.

67. Eliade, M. (1985). *A History of Religious Ideas, Volume 3: From Muhammad to the Age of Reforms.* (p. 88). Chicago: The University of Chicago Press.

68. *The New Testament of the New Jerusalem Bible.* Garden City: Image Books.

69. Mayer, H.E., (1988). *The Crusades.* (p. 11). Oxford: Oxford University Press.

70. *Ibid.*

71. *Ibid.*

72. *Ibid.*

73. Riley-Smith, J., (1987). *The Crusades: a Short History.* (p. 6) London: Yale University Press.

74. *The New Testament of the New Jerusalem Bible* (p. 28). Garden City: Image Books.

75. Mayer, H.E., (1988). *The Crusades.* (p. 11). Oxford: Oxford University Press.

76. Claster, J.N., (1982). *The Medieval Experience: 300-1400.* (p. 198). New York: New York University Press.

77. *Ibid.*

78. *Ibid.,* (p. 199).

79. *Ibid.*

80. *Ibid.*

81. *Crawford/Internet*

82. Claster, J.N., (1982). T*he Medieval Experience: 300-1400.* (p. 200). New York: New York University Press.

83. *Microsoft Encarta Encyclopedia.* (1996). Plague.

84. *Ibid.*

85. *Aids/Black Death/Internet*

86. *Ibid.*

87. Eliade, M. (1985) *A History of Religious Ideas, Volume 3: From Muhammad to the Age of Reforms.* (p. 206). Chicago: The University of Chicago Press.

88. Claster, J.N., (1982). *The Medieval Experience: 300-1400.* (p. 356). New York: New York University Press.

89. Eliade, M. (1985) *A History of Religious Ideas, Volume 3: From Muhammed to the Age of Reforms.* (p. 206). Chicago: The University of Chicago Press.

90. *Ibid.*

91. Rice, A. (1994).(*rice@ed.byu.edu*) I Saw the Death.

92. Claster, J.N., (1982). *The Medieval Experience: 300-1400.* (p. 359). New York: New York University Press.

93. Eliade, M. (1985) *A History of Religious Ideas, Volume 3: From Muhammed to the Age of Reforms.* (p. 236). Chicago: The University of Chicago Press.

94. *Ibid.,* (p.237).

95. *Ibid.*

96. *Ibid.*

97. Tuveson, E.L. (1972). *Millennium and Utopia.* (p. 22). Glouster: Peter Smith.

98. Armstrong, K. (1993). *A History of God.* (p. 275). New York: Ballantine Books.

99. *Ibid.*

100. *Ibid.,* (p. 276-277).

101. Tuveson, E.L. (1972). *Millennium and Utopia.* (p. 22). Glouster: Peter Smith.

102 *Ibid.*

103. *Ibid.,* (p. 24).

104. *Ibid.,* (p. 25).

105. *Ibid.*

106. *Ibid.,* (p. 26).

107. *Ibid.*

108. *Ibid.,* (p. 23).

109. *Ibid.,* (p. 26).

110. *Ibid.,* (p. 28).

111. *Ibid.,* (p. 29).

112. *Ibid.*

Apocalypse, final woodcut, Albrecht Dürer, 1498.

Chapter Five

The Millennium In America

*I*n people's minds the discovery of America was due to God's favor. It was part of His plan for a fresh beginning for mankind, in an age when most everything was starting anew. The New World myth did not ignore the older myths.

The myths that filled the minds and souls of the people on the Mayflower were the myths of Paradise, the Garden of Eden, and the Golden Age. The people transformed these ancient myths into what was to become the great myth of America.1

THE NEW WORLD

Myths precede discovery. Before the voyage of Columbus, others are reputed to have journeyed to the New World.[2] Leif Eiriksson is said to have landed in North America at the time of the first millennium, some five hundred years before Columbus. Four hundred years before that, Saint Brendan purportedly made the journey. There are additional records suggesting that the initial footprints placed on the sand of the Americas appeared twenty thousand years ago. This will be discussed later. Rollo May tells us in *The Cry for Myth* that before Columbus, Europeans simply were not ready for a mythical confrontation of this magnitude. Myth is resolute in what it will let people perceive, or ignore.[3]

Our picture of the intellectual, metaphysical, and religious climate of the Middle Ages shows a confined world that revolved around the Church, in hope and in faith that the suffering of this life would be transformed into joy in the next. The day to day world for most people was indeed a very small place, with most passing their entire lives within a fifty-mile radius of their homes.

In the pre-Columbian era, there were two basic visions of the earth in the universe. One view, over three thousand years old at the time, held that the earth was flat, afloat in the cosmos in the midst of dangerous monsters. This is the image of the world that is sanctioned by the Bible.[4] The more prevalent theory of the era was that the earth was an immobile sphere in the center of seven revolving spheres: the moon, the sun, Mercury, Venus, Mars, Jupiter, and

Saturn.[5] These seven bodies corresponded to the seven days of the week, with each day being named after one of them. A metal also corresponded with each body: silver, mercury, copper, gold, iron, tin, and lead.[6] As we make the journey from heaven to earth to be born among men, we absorb some of the traits of these substances, traits that are returned once we ascend, after death, to be judged by God. On earth, the Pope ruled in God's name. Clearly there was order and harmony in the universe[7], and as Campbell states:

"The Christian Empire was an earthly reflex of the order of the heavens, hieratically organized, with the vestments, thrones, and procedures of its stately courts inspired by celestial imagery, the bells of its cathedral spires and harmonies of its priestly choirs echoing in earthly tones the unearthly angelic hosts."[8]

The power of this confining scenario of existence over medieval society could only be broken by a movement of superior potency. That force, which started in the fourteenth century in Italy, is known to us as the Renaissance.[9] *Renaissance* is French for *rebirth,* which can be understood to mean, in the words of one historian, "the discovery of the world and of man."[10] For our purposes, to understand the gradual transition of medieval "inner"[11] thinking to the intellectual availability for consideration of a New World, it is particularly apt. The Renaissance "clearly was a time in which long standing beliefs were tested."[12]

If a date can be assigned to the transition between thinking with a Medieval perspective, to thinking with a modern vision of the world, perhaps it is 1492.[13] The old world and its Church-centered existence began to give way to the external, and to discovery. By discovery we not only refer to the accomplishments of Columbus, Magellan, and de Gama, but also to the discoveries in the arts, sciences, literature, and religion that were to follow. People began to take notice of the flurry of activity coming out of Italy, activity that portrayed life as more of an adventure to be experienced, an adventure that would challenge all boundaries, whether they be of the Church, of nature, or of the mind.[14] With this perspective, Europe was prepared to accept the discovery of a new world... "and to change the direction of their intentions and their dreams."[15]

We have described before the cyclical nature of existence that was espoused by the mythology of a variety of cultures. Depicted in these myths was an age that had grown decrepit from violence and sin, seemingly demanding its own conclusion, often by destruction. Following the dissolution of the old age, a new age is ushered in through the intervention of a cosmological figure.

An allegorical tale of the millennium can be found in the voyage of Columbus. His voyage marked the onset of a change in ages. He came from the decrepitude of Medieval Europe to Paradise, "a transfigured world."[16] The eschatological nature of this voyage, as well as his messianic role, was not lost on Columbus:

"It is I whom God had chosen for his messenger, showing me on which side were to be found the new heaven and new earth of which Isaiah had made previous mention."[17]

Regardless of how Columbus felt about himself or his voyage, he had to recognize that someone else had arrived in the "New World" first; the Native Americans.

THE NATIVE AMERICANS

If the arrival of Columbus in the New World changed European history forever, it also changed forever the lives of the Native Americans who greeted him. For them, the Americas did not represent Paradise or a new world to be conquered or plundered; for the natives, it was *home*.

Their home would never be the same again. The *two thousand* tribes that could be found in the Americas in the seventh century would dwindle to *three hundred* in the twentieth century.[18] This extinction was certainly due to the invasion of the Europeans, and their diseases, and was intensified by the bitter divisiveness between tribes, which precluded any meaningful or long term alliance, desperately needed measures against the atrocities of the immigrants.[19] The "native" in Native American is a literal fact among these cultures. Their mythology places their people in the Americas from their conception, not as migrants from some other continent. Scientific data estimates that these Americans have been "native" for about twenty thousand years.[20] Prior to that, there have been a variety of suggestions for the point of their origin; one claims the land/ice bridge between what is now known as Siberia and Alaska; another theory suggests Polynesia or Melanesia because of the similarities of cultivated plants, musical instruments, and other cultural artifacts.[21]

Perhaps the most dramatic example of the influence of other cultures on the Americas can be found in sacred buildings. The sacred building finds its roots in ancient Sumer around 3200 B.C.E.[22] By this date, many crucial cultural advances had been established: writing had been created, and by association, history had been established. The wheel was developed, and number systems were generated. A calendar of three hundred and sixty secular and five sacred days had been formulated. The five sacred days were those in which spiritual energy flowed from eternity to touch the earth. These days were imbued with rite, ritual, and celebration.[23]

The center of sacred space where the spiritual energy of the universe was believed to fuse with that of the earth was the *ziggurat*. The ziggurat was constructed in such a fashion that it correlated with the five sacred days. It had four sides, in synchronicity with the compass, and a platform at the top, a fifth aspect. On the platform stood a temple or shrine to receive the celestial energy or deity.[24] Temples of this type were named to describe their function. One such temple was simply named "Link Between Heaven and Earth."[25] What is so important about the ziggurat is that it served as a model that would be duplicated throughout the world. We can find the ziggurat blueprint in the Buddhist tradition of the towered city of Amaraviti, in the Greek Mount Olympus, and in the Aztec temples of the sun. There truly exists, it seems, a connection between cultures.

NATIVE AMERICAN ESCHATOLOGY

Despite twenty thousand years of presence, there is a dearth of sources of the Native American experience, because of the preliterate nature of many of the cultures. We have historical records of only the last four hundred years, with the majority of records having been written in only the *last hundred years*.[26] A paucity of data is not the only issue; another subject for concern is the objectivity of the records. The older sources are based on the commentary of Christian missionaries, whose impartiality toward Native Americans is questionable.[27] More recent sources record Native American cultures that have been massively exposed to the traditions, religions, and technology of Europe. This raises the concern of students and scholars regarding the purity of Native American religion and mythology. The question is whether our knowledge of the religious traditions is reflective of millennia of historical practice, or if we are witness to cultures and religions that include Christian elements.[28] Our interest concerns the possibility of a corresponding effect on Native American eschatology. The question of whether there is an ancient American tradition of belief in an afterlife, or whether this motif was absorbed by the tribes due to the assertive preaching of Christian missionaries is subject to debate. There are, however, some generalizations that can be made about Native American religious beliefs and their perceptions of life after death.[29]

Some Native American traditions are shared with other cultures and will be familiar to us. For example, at times determined to be culturally important, such as the transition from childhood to adulthood or preparations for the hunt, Native Americans pursued a link with the world of the spirits through *visions*.[30] This is now familiar to us as *rapture,* and this aspiration to connect with the spirit world was enacted in the wilderness. The child, seeking to cross the threshold into adult membership in the tribe, would pass several days in the wilderness with little or no food, water, or clothing. In this most submissive display before the spirits, the child lingered in anticipation of the vision, of the rapture.[31] If after several days the vision was not experienced, the child might determine that more self-sacrifice was necessary. The slicing of the skin or the amputation of a finger were among the possible recourses to assuage the spirits into a connection with the hopeful new adult.[32]

Besides rapture, Native Americans shared the nearly universal recognition of existence's cyclical nature; the understanding that all things have a beginning and an end, including existence itself. The notion of a world that has grown old, that requires a rebirth through its destruction, and that is followed by a new creation, is very much a part of many tribes' heritage, with the Aztecs being a primary example.[33] In some tribes, such as the Hupa, Yurok, the Hill, Plains Maidu, and Eastern Pomo from California, the creation of the world was reenacted regularly. This view perceived the world to always be at the brink of destruction, a fate avoided only by its ritual recreation.[34] This appears to be consistent with what we have described in Near Eastern eschatology.

Perhaps a perspective of the Native American view of death will help us understand the available remnants of their eschatological views. With two thousand tribes and the resultant diversity of ideas, it is important to understand that there was never one single Native American view on any particular topic.[35] However, there are some general inferences that can be made.

Native American tradition dictated that the dead should be handled with care and caution. Mishandling the dead could result in their return to the world of the living, where they would cause trouble. Interestingly, this fear represented Native Americans' major concern about death. Eyewitnesses such as missionaries have recorded that when facing their own individual death, Native Americans were remarkable for their *lack of fear*.[36]

Apparently Native Americans presumed that each individual possessed two souls, neither of which was regarded as immortal. The living breath of the physical body was considered to be one soul; upon the corruption that follows the death of the body, this soul dies.[37] The other soul was not attached to the body. This soul had the autonomy to roam during dreams or to remove itself from the body during illness. Upon the death of the body, this soul proceeded to the land of the dead.[38]

The land of the dead is not a well described place in Native American tradition. In many traditions, there exists no difficulty in describing the afterlife. Whether from sacred texts or other sources, powerful images are used to construct the magical paradise of heaven, the horrible terrors of hell, or simply the everyday life in the other world. Some Native American tribes have described the land of the dead as a place of contentment, while others describe it as an abode of sadness. The land of the dead is also depicted as a resumption of this life "on another plane of existence."[39]

There appears to be no distinction made regarding who goes to this land following their death, as all the dead seem destined to journey there. There is no heaven for the good, nor a hell for the evil. How the deceased were prepared for their trip to the land of the dead seems to have depended upon their importance. Burial with food and drink was not uncommon, while others with more status might be buried with a guide. The chieftains of the Natchez in Mississippi were accompanied by many. Wives, children, friends, and animals gave up their own lives, or requested them sacrificed, to make the journey with a person of such authority.[40] The similarity between this tradition and the burial rites of rulers of other cultures, such as the Egyptian pharaohs, is remarkable.

In Native American tradition, we have said, the soul is not immortal; so consequently, its time in the land of the dead was not eternal. A very poignant perspective on time is offered instead. The soul lasts only as long as memories of the soul exist in the hearts and minds of the living. But as the memories of the living fade, or the keepers of the memory die, the soul starts to fade. Upon the passing of the last memory, when the soul is forever erased from the mind, it disappears from the land of the dead.[41]

We have been witness to other cultures' myths of destruction by fire or flood, as with the Huichol, and sometimes fire *and* flood. The eschatological fire scenario referred to as "universal combustion" appears in the tradition of the Yucatan Mayas, as well as the Aztecs of Mexico.[42] The Aztecs perceived the present world as the fifth world, or fifth Sun, called Ollin, or movement. Their tradition tells them that four worlds have preceded the present one, with the fate of all the previous worlds sealed by catastrophe.[43] The Aztecs, an extremely sophisticated civilization, calculated and divided time into periods of numerous cycles lasting fifty-two years. Larger periods, the suns, were made of numerous fifty-two year cycles. At the end of one of these larger periods of fifty-two, their present world would end with a great shaking. Their computations indicate 2007 as that year.[44]

Hopi tradition has the present world as being the fourth world. The following myth describes the evolution from the first to the fourth world. The first world was populated by insects. This world was not satisfactory to Tawa, the Sun Spirit and creator, because insects do not understand life's meaning.[45] He required them to journey upward to a second world. During this journey, the insects transformed into animals, who also do not understand life's meaning. Still not satisfied, Tawa sent the animals up to a third world. On this journey some of the animals became people. Men and women were taught survival skills, and with the passage of time began to understand the meaning of life.[46]

After some time, the message of the meaning of life was lost as men and women fell under the influence of evil *powaka,* or sorcerers, and became sinful and neglected their children. Tawi was displeased with his people. It was time to journey up to a new world.[47] After much difficulty, the great climb upward to the new, current world was accomplished. And as people arrived, they were divided into the different tribes: Hopi, Navajo, Apache, and so on. The evil powaka were unable to finish the climb and fell to the world below. Those who were successful in their climb knew that they had to share this world with the resident awaiting their arrival-*Masuwu,* the Hopi word for death.[48] Hopi cosmology dictates the existence of nine worlds overall. The time left for the present, fourth world, is said to be brief. A fifth world will follow this one.[49]

The Hopi originate from the American southwest, specifically from Northeastern Arizona, where they lived in pueblos. Their ancient village of *Oraibi* is considered the spiritual center of the world. The Hopi see the world as a place where spirituality is absent from all, save themselves.[50] The Hopi see the need for the emergence of a fifth world, because they believe that much of the present world will be destroyed by nuclear weapons. The Hopi lands, however, will survive unscathed. They maintain that there is no benefit in building shelters, because evil can never be sheltered. But all who strive against divisiveness, regardless of race, will have a place in the next world.[51]

The next war will be started, the Hopi say, by an older culture, such as Egypt, China, India, or Palestine. They further indicate that both World War I and II were accurately anticipated by their culture. They say that for those who care to look, the earth itself is preparing for the transition to the fifth world. It can be seen in the disenfranchised peoples all over the world, and it can be seen in the earth, in the planets, and in the stars. And, the Hopi say, it can be seen in our hearts.[52]

Native Americans are renowned for their symbiosis with nature. They believe that all parts of nature, even the most humble, deserve the respect of men. This special understanding of the ways of nature and the meaning of its cycles, allows Native Americans a comfort where others experience fear. Whether it be as personal as one's own death, or as universal as the end of existence, there is an acceptance, even an optimism, on the part of Native Americans that is steeped in the wisdom of the powerful simplicity that the end is normal, and most importantly, is never irrevocable.[53]

THE PURITANS

Martin Luther, overcome with fury at a Church that was in the business of selling redemption and a God that was impossible to please, launched the Reformation in Wittenberg, Germany in 1517. His action would provide the impetus for religious reforms and revolutions for more than a century to follow. For all the power of his scholarship and his urgency to come to an understanding with his God, Luther was never able to calm the emotional storm that raged inside him. The enduring gift that is bestowed upon those who have the good fortune to attain true insight, "peace, serenity, and loving kindness" was, for some reason, tragically denied him. The anger resulting from his frustration drove Luther to reform, but it also caused many potential followers to keep their distance.[54] There was a much more favorable reception to the reform promulgated by John Calvin.

Calvin was a sixteenth century revisionist who, at one time, was completely fascinated with the splendor of the Church hierarchy and the papacy. He experienced a total metamorphosis from this feeling when it became clear to him that this very hierarchy was nothing but an impediment to the sacred connection between the individual soul and God.[55] Among the obstructing intermediaries were the saints, whom Calvin claimed were worshipped out of a sense of anxiety. This feeling was generated by a fear of further angering an already wrathful God. The faithful felt that God's wrath could be softened by "gaining the ear of those closest to Him."[56] Under Calvinism, this anxiety was turned into an outright rejection of the saints as additional hindrances to direct access to God. This rejection was manifested in hostility and violence, as statues of the saints and the virgin were shattered and smashed, and frescoes in churches and cathedrals were whitewashed.[57] Calvin's followers felt an extreme frustration with years of interference with the simple act of worship, and this frustration was darkly demonstrated.

The construct of Calvinism that is probably most familiar to us is *predestination*. Predestination states that God in His mystery has determined from His eternal perspective that some of us are fated for salvation, while the rest of us are doomed to damnation. This view was not seminal to Calvin's doctrine during his lifetime. It achieved prominence after his death (1564) as a point of difference to distinguish Calvinists from both Lutherans and Roman

Catholics.[58]

The Calvinistic perspective was the basis of the religious experience of the Puritans. A significant burden that was part of a Puritan's daily existence was contending with the overwhelming concept of predestination, "and a terror that they would not be saved."[59] For these devout people, there was a tremendous preoccupation with the potential disdain of a God who at times seemed devoid of mercy. This burden of omnipresent oppression begot cases of clinical depression and suicide. These darknesses in the human psyche were, naturally, assigned to the darkest of powers, Satan. Satan was perceived to be a formidable power present in the daily lives of the Puritan faithful.[60] This observation of the presence and availability of dark powers in the routine existence of men and women would culminate in the tragedy of the Salem witch trials. The excessive pressure of being a Puritan resulted in a constant sense of dread, and bigotry directed toward those who were not Puritans.[61] A simple quote from the era might be of assistance in clarification: "We call you Puritans not because you are purer than other men, but because you think yourselves to be purer."[62]

The Church of England was facing its own crisis in the early sixteenth century. In his dispute with the pope over his right to marry, Henry VIII seized authority over the English faithful for himself, effectively terminating the authority of Rome.[63] Those who thought that Henry's seizure of ecclesiastical command in England would provide favorable change for the devoted were to be terribly disappointed. The evils that were identified with the papacy still thrived.

Many members of the clergy directed their attention to matters more financial than spiritual. Matters of holiness and the well-being of the soul tended to be focused upon the landlords, who owned the land upon which the members of the clergy lived, and were responsible for the clergy's income. The clergy's lack of spirituality is evident, in that it was common for the clergy to be unfamiliar with the Bible, even to the point of being incapable of reciting the Ten Commandments. The pursuit of multiple incomes, impunity of the law, raw ignorance, literal as well as spiritual corruption, and fealty to Rome are only a few of the transgressions that fueled the enmity between the clergy and the faithful.[64]

In reaction, the observer will find that as the sixteenth century progressed, small amounts of reform stimulated the desire for more.

This resulted in a state of spiritual/political affairs that found the monarchy continually assailed with demands for changes in the church's rites, rituals, and ethics.[65] The constant dissatisfaction of the Puritans, who zealously pursued the cleansing or "purifying" of their faith from the faults of England's spiritual establishment, began to try the patience of the monarchy. Even the diplomacy of Queen Elizabeth I was insufficient to satisfy the Puritans. By 1577, Elizabeth had exhausted the depths of her patience. She decreed that participation in the Church of England include only the rite and ritual of the Church of England. The effect of this message was to effectively drive the Puritans, and their unceasing demands, underground by the end of the century.[66] The term "Puritan" became commensurate with "radical." An attempt by the established clergy to foster a climate of conciliation with the Puritans in the beginning of the seventeenth century was extinguished by James VI. The monarch correctly perceived that a radical group who resisted the authority of the church hierarchy would eventually be resistant to his authority as well. His response was: "I will harry them out of the land."[67]

THE PURITANS AND THE MILLENNIUM

During the seventeenth century in England, there were a number of circumstances that provided the means for the Puritan community to enthusiastically embrace millennarianism. At this time, the writings of Augustine were twelve centuries old. Augustine was still esteemed as one of the Church's preeminent writers. He considered the millennium in Revelations as an allegory for the reign of the Church, a figurative image of time. The millennium, Augustine interpreted, was an image of time so remote that it was outside even the most distant perception of history.[68] But Luther's interpretation of Revelations was that perhaps Augustine's millennium was now well overdue, since it was 1200 years later, meaning that the end of days could occur at any time. This view was bolstered by the fact that since Luther's action at Wittenberg, the pace of activities and circumstances, both religious and political, left many Puritans believing that history was "hurtling toward its final act."[69]

Luther was an originator of the trend of attempting to match the events of the day with the images of Revelations to determine if the millennium was at hand. The trend caught on, and the Puritans were among those to view their contemporary history through the lenses of Revelations. The prediction of history's demise began to be practiced by many, each professing a singular gift for this craft. Among the prognosticators of the era was the immensely talented poet John Milton, whose *Paradise Lost* concludes with the revelation of an angel to Adam and Eve. The entire future history of mankind is revealed to the Biblical first man and woman. The angel concludes the disclosure with the events of the end of days.[70] By the mid-seventeenth century, the perception that the end of the world was unfolding was accepted by Puritans as simple fact.[71]

In a previous chapter, we have discussed the relationship between the occurrence of a disaster and the formation of a millennarian movement. Disaster can be manifested as the product of a calamity of nature, such as a flood, or as an act of terrorism. But, according to Barkun, disaster need not be so obviously destructive. It can refer to any radical changes in the environment, and radical change, like beauty, is apparently in the eye of the beholder.[72] The changes can slowly occur over a long period, or quite suddenly. The Puritans saw their environment changing rapidly, observing change after change in the crisis ridden religious-political world of the late sixteenth and early seventeenth centuries.[73]

The Puritans present an interesting and unusual profile compared to most millennarian movements. Millennarian movements, as we will see, typically enlist or attract supporters possessed of little formal education. This, however, was not the case with the Puritans. Their movement was populated with sophisticated and well-educated ministers, merchants, and lawyers.[74] But as with many other groups, the Puritans viewed the society in which they existed as religiously and politically disastrous, and quite beyond redemption.[75] Their response was to turn their back on this society, and they were rejected in return. They decided to look elsewhere to practice their faith as they desired, and that place was America. America, in the millennial fervor of the seventeenth century, became the New Jerusalem.

The Puritans, self-anointed as God's select, confidently awaited His judgement on their political and religious oppressors.[76] The arrival of the millennium, as well as God's favor, however, could be hastened by following the directive given to the Apostles. That directive was to spread the Gospel to all corners of the earth, no matter how remote.[77] America was the perfect locale for an oppressed religious group, especially one intensely preoccupied with their place in the end of days scenario, which they believed was very much at hand. New England would become, the Puritans thought, a community of the spiritual select, a gathering place of the chosen to await the coming of the Lord.[78]

Perhaps from a sense of guilt over the oppressive measures they exercised on Native Americans, who were willing to share the New World's bountiful resources as well as their own possessions, the Puritans expended substantial effort in justifying colonization. They persuaded themselves that in exchange for what they stole from Native Americans, the colonists were providing the much more valuable gift of the Gospel.[79] There were other justifications developed for colonization. One was the Biblical directive "to be fruitful and multiply," a second was that a summons from God had been answered, and yet another mused that young people leave home when they marry, anyway. There was also the interpretation that it was sinful to unnecessarily endure a life of hardship and misery in the Old World, and allow the God-given gift of the New World to go to waste. The analogy of bees leaving an overpopulated hive to establish a new one was also employed to illustrate the natural process of colonization.[80]

As the Puritans settled in New England, we find at this location more than at any other colony, ongoing activities directed at preparing for the millennium. In the very crossing of the ocean to arrive at the Massachusetts Bay Colony, the Puritans perceived themselves to be engaged in a journey of Biblical proportions, a journey commensurate with the Old Testament exodus of the Jews. But this time, the destination was the New Jerusalem.[81]

And for the many who looked, there were ample signs that the millennium was at hand. Samuel Sewall, a chronicler of events that pointed toward the millennium, saw the great earthquake of Lima in 1687 as a sign right out of Revelations.[82] Preaching to the natives took on an urgency which was spurred by the feeling that the sooner the Gospel was spread, the sooner Christ would return. Native Americans were informed of the role they had in hastening the Second Coming by their acceptance of the Gospel. Other signs were duly noted. A comet is said to have passed over America, passing from east to west just prior to the arrival of the Puritans. This spectacular event was followed some time later by a darker occurrence: a plague that substantially reduced the Native American population.[83]

Having settled in the New World, the Puritans set about the business of practicing their faith free of hierarchical and ritualistic distraction. The congregation itself became an imposing power. They were now unfettered as they contended with the tremendous dilemma of being a Puritan: to live a perfect life in a world that is imperfect, undertaking a pursuit that could only guarantee failure.[84] Their understandable frustration with an impossible circumstance may have created a change in attitude. It appears that by the 1670s, a perceptible change could be observed in the Puritan population of the Massachusetts Bay Colony. The feeling that the end of times was near had not changed. What had changed was the spiritual deportment of the Puritans, those self-anointed select who felt that they stood to be favored by the arrival of the Second Coming.

This attitude was of great concern to the Reverend Increase Mather, a renowned spiritual leader and historical figure in the history of Massachusetts Bay and the City of Boston. The Reverend Mather sensed a self-comfort, self-satisfaction, and complacency in his congregation. His observations propelled him to deliver a series of *jeremiads*, or warning sermons. These presentations are named for the Old Testament prophet Jeremiah, whose writings included the importance of individual responsibility in the relationship between God and man. Jeremiads served to call upon God's wrath to obtain the attention of His sinful people.[85] The phrase "fire and brimstone" best describes the content of a jeremiad.

In his sermons, the Reverend Mather reminded his flock that the end of days was near, because one biblical sign of those days was "wars and rumors of wars."[86] Wars and rumors of wars were most certainly heard in 1674, as they have been heard in almost any other year in world history. As the sermon continued, the Reverend Mather insisted to his parishioners that they were living under "a cloud of blood."[87] He was trying, through the use of a little terror, to rid his flock of the arrogant perception that they would be saved. The terror that he infused in his sermon would ebb, just as the religious zeal of the Puritans had over the one-half century they had remained in the New World.

The business of constructing a colony, a New Jerusalem, became big business. There was money to be made, which held an earthly but powerful distraction from the realm of the spiritual. Boston became an economic hub, and the children of the Puritans began to select the "good life" as opposed to the "godly life."[88] A quote from the era may illustrate a change of heart: "It may be the last and great coming of the Lord is not very nigh..."[89] By the time of the American Revolution, the Puritans were the establishment, and Puritans would see their zealous thunder stolen by a number of new radical sects, established by new sets of societal and spiritual rules created by war and ever expanding frontiers.

While "Puritan" certainly has its negative connotations, we need to remind ourselves that the Puritan legacy continues to thrive in America today, even for those who do not practice a religion or even believe in a god.[90] The Puritan work ethic continues to propel the American economy. To this day, the Puritan notion of being select, or chosen, in God's eyes is powerfully entrenched in the American psyche.[91]

PRECURSORS TO REVOLUTION

In eighteenth century America, there were a number of social, religious, and political forces present that had a significant impact on the consciousness of the colonists. Combined, these circumstances created a powerful force of resistance to the authority of England, ultimately leading to the American Revolution. This revolution, according to John Adams, had occurred in the minds and hearts of the people a generation before Lexington and Concord in 1775.[92]

The first half of the eighteenth century found the colonies, some now more than one hundred years old, busily engaged in the business of economic growth and geographic expansion. The east coast of the colonies could no longer be described as wilderness as the development of seaports and corresponding economic activity promulgated the creation of settlements that expanded into towns, and blossomed into cities. So rapid and so great was the development of the colonies that for some residents of the New World, there were too many similarities with the worn and weary towns and cities of England. Correspondingly, there was concern that the Old World preoccupation with monetary gain had also traversed the Atlantic Ocean. With this realization, colonists were concerned that the intensity of faith was weakened, and the special promise of the New World was tarnished and broken. Most importantly, there was a growing fear that God's spirit had been withdrawn from the colonies.[93]

In order to renew what was felt to be a special spiritual relationship between God and the colonies, some enthusiasm had to be introduced in the religious life of the colonists in order to revive it from its dormant state. There was an urgency to this spiritual predicament, because it was felt that the residents of the New World had to be held to a higher standard. This notion would find its label in literature that portrayed the colonies as the *American Israel.* The New World was different than the Old World, and demanded a new religion, one demonstrating a dramatic change over past practice, "which affected the hearts and emotions of the people."[94] This "new religion" was to depend highly upon emotion and emotional response, which represented a substantial change from the mostly staid presentation of the clergy and passive participation of the parishioners that were familiar at the time.[95] This change in view was consistent with the philosophy of the Enlightenment, the eighteenth century movement of thought that challenged the idea that the value of one's beliefs was somehow correlated to the age of those beliefs. Under an Enlightenment perspective, the principles of the past were no longer the stanchion of veracity and dependability they were presumed to be.[96]

THE GREAT AWAKENING

The descriptor given to this wave of evangelical enthusiasm is *The Great Awakening.* The easiest way to describe the events of the Great Awakening is through the picture of a revival. By experience or observation, most of us are familiar with a religious revival meeting. The picture illustrates an accomplished preacher, gifted with words, and physically demonstrative. The congregation is seemingly consumed in the moment, moved by two forces, their inner faith and the charisma of the preacher. These forces cause members of the congregation to move to the music of their feelings with a tempo found either within the worshiper or in the melody of the preacher's rhetorical meter. Caught in the enthusiasm of the moment, the participants feel the freedom to confess wrongdoings or to lavish praise on God. This contemporary image has its roots in the Great Awakening of the pre-Revolutionary era.

In 1739 Massachusetts, Jonathan Edwards, called our greatest theologian by Harold Bloom, hoped that the millennium would soon commence in the New World.[97] He invited a young preacher from England named George Whitefield to come to America. In an extremely successful series of sermons delivered along the coast of the colonies, Whitefield gathered large numbers of people wherever he went, as his gift for language and dramatic delivery generated much enthusiasm among his audiences. Whitefield became the father of revivalism in this country, having an extremely successful "tour", and has been called the first person in this country to whom the designation "star" can be applied.[98]

The Great Awakening represented the interesting contrast of an orthodox religion being dispensed radically through affect and theater. Advocates of the Awakening defended the unconventional methodology by observing that the uncommon times dictated unusual approaches for the maintenance of a privileged relationship with God. In addition, the advocates felt, the special nature and unique promise of the New World generated the notion that God works in unusual ways. To its supporters, the Great Awakening and its corresponding emotional upheaval were external symbols of the beneficence of the flow of the goodness of God.[99] Retrospectively, observers of this era would assign to the Awakening the focus of the American millennial anticipation of the times, as well as a provocation for the American Revolution.[100]

The Great Awakening was seen as the dawn of a new era, a period of revival, a regeneration of religious fervor. Part of the agenda of this movement was the accomplishment of numerous conversions, which was believed to hasten the arrival of the millennium.[101] Inspired by the gifted Whitefield, new standards had been set for preaching, and charismatic wordsmiths traveled the colonies, touting the dawn of a new day, a new Reformation, the promise of Revelations.

The power of preaching is not unknown to us. In our contemporary culture, we place much value on those whose craft with words is persuasive, if not mesmerizing. The sublime talents of those such as the Reverend Jesse Jackson, or former Governor Mario Cuomo are among the few in political life whose words are anticipated, not dreaded. There are also "motivational" speakers who have become quite wealthy because of the quality of their ability to combine expression of the highest caliber that somehow manages to strike an emotional chord in the listener. There of course is also a danger in the power of words. In 1930's Germany, Hitler was able to convince many of the benefits of his ideas. Even the wise and talented, such as Carl Jung, were temporarily fooled by the power of the tyrant's words. Samuel Adams was right. People are governed more by their feelings than by reason.[102]

Contemporary parallels still fall short of describing the power of preaching in colonial America during the Great Awakening. We live in a media saturated society. Newspapers, magazines, books, telephones, radio, television, computers, and the internet all provide us with the information we need when we need it. In 1740 colonial America, with the exception of a few poorly circulated newspapers, the information of the day came through preaching.[103] And as in any art, preaching had talented, even exceptional practitioners, whose power would soon be felt in an agenda that was not entirely spiritual.

During this era, the Baptists started their impressive growth by breaking with Protestant convention and advocating for lay preachers. The importance of this innovation was far reaching. The power of the pulpit was now available to all who desired it, and in a society where preaching had the clout of a major medium, this was considerable power indeed.[104] In this era, the pulpit, whether it be in a church or on the town common, was not simply a forum for the spiritual maintenance of the congregation. It was also a platform for challenge to the establishment of the day, whether it be the religious forces adversarial to the emotional aura of the Awakening, or the political events born from the tyranny of England. This challenge of the establishment, regardless of its source, was a watershed for a movement for change.[105] The heady mix of issues, both political and spiritual, that were emanating from the pulpit, clouded the line of separation between the sacred and the secular. Sacred issues such as the millennium would soon become civil matters, and governmental matters such as independence assumed a mantle of holiness.[106]

RELIGIOUS FOUNDATION FOR REVOLUTION

In the lofty self-perception as being God's chosen in a Promised Land, the colonists were possessed of a conviction that the New World was *theirs*. Thus it is no surprise to discover that the powers of England and France, both of who had substantial interests in

America, were viewed with growing hostility. In the spiritual revival born of the Awakening, the promise of an impending millennium was also rekindled. As this apocalyptic event was discussed, the identification of the Anti-Christ was easily determined. Followers of Protestantism could always find the Anti-Christ in Rome, where under various names, he had lived for quite some time.[107] Any dark circumstance that could befall Catholicism, and by connection, the Pope, was seen as a defeat for the Anti-Christ. This was the perspective employed at the conclusion of the French and Indian War in 1763. The defeat of the Catholic French by the Protestant English was taken as an apocalyptic defeat for the Anti-Christ/Pope.[108] However, the failure of the millennium to transpire at the end of this conflict suggested that another Anti-Christ was extant. The power of England was now a fresh target for tyrannical labels because of a series of rapidly occurring events that intensified the already burgeoning resistance of the colonists.

Over the years, the number of Episcopalians in New England had enlarged. The number was substantial enough to raise the issue of whether bishops needed to be brought in from England to tend this growing flock. This seemingly innocuous expression on the part of some worshipers sparked nothing less than a furious response from colonists of other sects. Still fresh in the minds of some colonists were the accounts of the executions and persecutions on the part of Catholic bishops in the Old World. The fact that the persecutors were Catholic, and not Episcopalian, was deemed irrelevant. Bishops of any ilk were now suspect, because the imposition of these church officials, the colonists concluded, would only serve as a precursor for other English interference.[109]

The fear of further interference was well founded. Following the expense of winning the French and Indian War in 1763, the English were very much interested in obtaining finances from the colonists themselves for the ten thousand troops stationed in the colonies. The Stamp Tax and the Townshend Acts were examples of the measures produced in England to raise revenue. Needless to say, the colonists resisted, with resulting riots and, in 1770, the Boston Massacre produced five dead colonists, killed by British rifles. In a fusion of rage of the clergy and the citizenry, liberty became an issue with paramount spiritual and civil status. The horrible beast of Revelations was now transformed into the English army.[110] In 1775, the American Revolution began at Lexington and Concord. The war would last eight long years until the treaty of 1783. During this period, thoughts of the millennium were never far from the minds of many colonists. The war and its tribulations generated apocalyptic images. The Declaration of Independence was seen as a "decree promulgated from heaven." The civil and sacred millennium offered the promise of the Kingdom of God, and the gift of liberty at the same time.[111]

The anticipation of the achievement of independence from the British Crown was seen as the commencement of a new history, for a new nation with seemingly infinite land to the west to serve as heaven on earth.[112] All of the above served as themes much too tempting to be ignored by the preachers of the day, as the images of the impending Apocalypse were illuminated time and again.[113] Along the way, the preachers received a little assistance from the heavens to make their case, on the Dark Day of 1780.

THE DARK DAY OF 1780

By 1780, the revolution had already raged for five long years. And as with all wars, the revolution exacted its price, to be paid in the currency of anguish, blood, death, and destruction. Observers of the times sought signs of the coming millennium in the social, spiritual, and political events around them, seeking to match them with Revelation images. On May 19, 1780, nature provided a spectacle that was seen as nothing less than an omen from God in the Last Days.

On this day most of New England experienced intense darkness during hours when daylight would ordinarily prevail. Reports that followed this extraordinary event were uniformly indicative of the uncanny absence of light. Some indicated that it was too dark to read, others stated that it was so dark that animals retired as if it were night, and people were forced to eat by candlelight. That there was darkness when there should have been light seems to have been consistently reported. Embellishments on the original story such as the appearance of "balls of fire" are probably less reliable.[114]

For the many people predisposed to the connection between the war and the impending millennium, the occurrence of the Dark Day had repercussions that would be hard for us to appreciate. In his brief but fascinating account of the day, Marini calls the impact "electric."[115] Another report, this one from a Revolutionary war fifer, recalls "the day as dark as night," and "people out wringing their hands and howling, 'the day of judgement is come.'"[116] Whether actual witness to the event, or recipient of the reports that followed, the Dark Day generated more than a little trepidation. The biblically erudite of the period, and there were many, did not need to be reminded that the only other times such an event transpired was during the tribulations visited upon the Egyptians in the time of the Exodus, and at the moment of Christ's death.[117] These were historical and spiritual milestones, circumstances whose import demanded the active intervention of God through the sign of darkness. The conclusion to be drawn about the significance of the War for Independence, for those who wished to make one, was obvious. Even for those less certain that this event was Apocalyptic, they nonetheless took pause and noticed the power of God.

The reverberations of the shock of the Dark Day of 1780 did not dissipate as the darkness did on the following day. Its importance as an eschatological sign continued well into the nineteenth century for the Seventh Day Adventists, and references to this occurrence can be found on the internet today. The cause of the Dark Day is unclear. Espoused theories include eclipses, and smoke from land clearing fires[118], a common activity in preparing the wilderness for "civilization."

REVOLUTION/ MILLENNIUM

The horror of war is a constant, regardless of the political or religious aura that surrounds or propels it. As with all wars, the American Revolution threw the colonies into a state of chaos, consuming materials and monetary resources built over many years. Institutions such as the Congregationalist churches would not recuperate until some years after the war, in 1790.[119]

The discord and tumult caused by the war, and the reconstruction that followed its conclusion, created a population shift. Thousands of people moved from the heavily populated areas proximate to the coast of New England, to unpopulated areas in Maine, Vermont, and New Hampshire.[120] This large scale immersion into the wilderness introduced a literal and philosophical break from the socio-cultural mainstream of the colonies. The war period from 1778-1782 found intense millennial anticipation in the wilderness communities. Religious enthusiasm surrounded the preachings of "prophets" such as Ann Lee, the founder of the Shakers. With the Revolutionary War, we are witness to the culmination of over one hundred and fifty years of colonial dissent often expressed in millennial terms.

Barkun's association of revolution and millennarianism begins with an understanding of the term *revolution*. Revolution, he tells us, finds its origins in astronomical terms, familiar to us as a descriptor for a rotational motion around a point. Over time, it had a metaphorical connotation as a change in a political system with accompanying violence; further associations would reduce the term to a referent to any change. Rebellion, a related term, also has violent roots, but does not essentially change the political status quo.[121]

Revolution and millennarianism, are, it seems, very closely linked. Social discontent demands a stage for performance. This platform can be constructed from either secular or sacred planks. A platform constructed from sacred planks will provide a millennarian performance, while a secular base will produce revolution. The distinction, Barkun states, is largely artificial.[122] Hence, in the American Revolution, the religious imagery of the coming of the millennium was painted with the political issues of liberty and freedom.[123] John Adams saw political America as a "...new continent in God's hands for great and gracious purposes."[124]

Barkun states: "...most events we now regard as revolutions took place after Western society had become secularized, and as a result, social discontent was expressed in secular terms." However, he indicates, the messiahism in revolution lives on.[125] Moorhead, in his wonderful study of the civil war, *American Apocalypse,* agrees. "The weaving of secular and religious motifs into one holy history became commonplace after independence."[126]

THE GREAT DISAPPOINTMENT

The American Revolution was a triumph for the commitment to the ideals of both political and religious freedom. In this new land, there was a prominent affirmation of the evangelical experience for both the individual and the nation. Through religious practice and the conversion of even more to the fold, it was felt that the dual promise of "national virtue and national unity" could be attained.[127] National unity, however, would be short lived, as the question of the hypocrisy of slavery in a free country would be asked with growing vehemence. National virtue was also subject to dissension, with the preponderance of new "visions and experiments for the future."[128]

The keeper of one of these visions was William Miller. Miller was born in 1782. Although his mother was the daughter of a Baptist preacher, Miller was disinterested in Christianity. As a soldier in the war of 1812, he was impressed by the fact that despite the lack of morality in his fellow soldiers, the virtuous cause of America allowed it to prevail against the British. His conclusion was that God had somehow invested Himself in the destiny of the United States. After the war, he developed the conviction that his relationship with God required his attention. Miller proceeded to immerse himself in Bible study for fourteen years.[129] The result of this undertaking, which served to make Miller a historical figure, is that through a series of calculations, he became convinced that the Second Coming of Christ would occur soon. The Bible is replete with the assignment of time periods, for both the life spans of some of its figures, as well as for durations of events. Depending on one's acceptance of literal versus symbolic applications of these numbers, a variety of dates for the Second Coming could be calculated. Miller's interpretation and mathematics provided him with the year 1843. By 1831, Miller felt "called by God" to preach his discovery,[130] and he was not without listeners. At one point he was attributed to have 100,000 followers.[131]

As 1843 approached, Miller's well-publicized prediction received even more attention. On January 1, 1843, Miller set the time frame as between March 21, 1843, and March 21, 1844. By the beginning of 1844, the Second Coming had not arrived, but the impassioned preaching of believers continued to arouse the populace. During this time, physicians were heard to be concerned about the rise in patients' suffering from this "delusion."[132]

March 21, 1844 came and went without event. Yet another date was set, October 22, 1844. As the some of the faithful patiently awaited their destiny, others were more dramatic in their preparatory activities; homes were left, possessions sold, and a pilgrimage to the mountains undertaken.[133] But October 22, 1844 passed without consequence.

Many of the followers were devastated. Besides the heartbreak experienced from their tireless efforts on behalf of a movement that came to naught, they were victimized by a cruel and ridiculing public. It was the Great Disappointment.

The Great Disappointment provides us with a look at what happens to prophecies that fail. Following the failure of its prophecy, Millerism dissolved. However, some followers regrouped and declared that the prophecy *did* occur. The locale of the occurrence was heaven. The Second Coming on earth was still imminent, they maintained, but its precise date should not be set by mankind. This group thrives to this day as the Seventh Day Adventists.[134]

THE CIVIL WAR

The victory over the British in the Revolutionary War provided, as wars frequently do, spoils. The 1783 Treaty of Paris, marking the formal end to the war provided the cherished gift of independence. Another benefit was the acquisition of land west to the Mississippi, providing ample land for expansion, and a new wilderness to conquer. In 1803, the Louisiana Purchase would provide 800,000 square miles of additional territory for the continued growth of this young and promising democracy. This seemingly limitless land that stretched out before Americans was lush with the potential of dreams to be fulfilled, utopias to be created, and refuges to await the Second Coming. America during this period was, as it still is, a magnet that draws dreamers and their followers to bask in the freedom to heed whatever call they have heard.[135]

The era of the Civil War was filled with those attentive to a Second Coming, groups akin to the Millerites just presented. In religious enclaves, fervent discussions about Biblical chronology and temporal progression were engaged in with relish. Two newspapers of the era, the *Prophetic Times* and the *Christian Intelligencer*, devoted themselves to providing their readers with information about perspectives for the timetable for the millennium.[136] While these newspapers did not have the imprimatur of mainstream Protestantism,[137] they did generate a readership.

The events of the day were applied to the *Book of Revelations* with liberal interpretations. Moorhead, in his detailed analysis *American Apocalypse: Yankee Protestants and the Civil War 1860-1869*, recounts some extrapolations of the age. A Brooklyn preacher, L. S. Weed, surveyed the squabbles in Congress, and the wars and rebellions in Europe. In the style of the tried and true "wars and rumors of wars" trigger for the Second Coming, Weed went to the Bible for further illumination. Turning to the *Book of Daniel*, Weed determined that the prophesied "fifth and universal empire" to succeed the declining Europe, must be America. Looking to *Revelations,* the preacher saw the engagement of angels with Satan, as analogous to the conflict of Union vs. Confederacy. The Confederacy, he maintained, was doomed to defeat. Following this event, subsequent skirmishes would dominate the landscape of the world, with the final outcome being the worldwide acceptance of the Gospels and American democracy.[138]

The Civil War, according to Weed, was nothing less than a central occurrence in the entire history of the world. Nor was he alone in his feelings. Moorhead recounts other examples of the impassioned, who might not have agreed with Weed's details, but certainly agreed with him in substance. God's "model Israel," the United States, was set, through the elimination of slavery, to presage the millennium.[139]

The issues that were behind the Civil War provided a reprise of the climate of the Revolutionary War, in the sense that the sacred and the secular were once again blurred. There were appeals to acquiesce to the "government of God."[140] This view defined the Christian call, an impetus to care for the congregation, certainly, but an additional responsibility to tend the "direction and functioning of the entire social system."[141]

As the war clouds thickened in the years following 1850, the shining light of optimism that appeared to shine on the mission of America dimmed into depression. The Fugitive Slave Act of 1850, which required the return of escaped slaves, the publishing of Uncle Tom's Cabin, and the Dred Scott Decision, which ruled that slaves had no rights before a court of law, were among the woeful realities of the era. John Brown's Raid was also a product of the time. It exemplified the passion over slavery, a passion so intensely felt that it drove citizens to murder. The pain found in the issue of slavery was becoming intolerable.[142]

The millennium that was coming with the Civil War, it was warned, bore the magic of the ultimate promise, and the scourge of a maximal threat. A Golden Age awaited the chosen nation that came to the millennium with justice in its heart. But the failure to keep the gleam on its promise would provide the reason for the visitation of tribulations.[143] The coming of the millennium had its adherents and its detractors, its faithful and its cynics. The Battle of Fort Sumter on April 12, 1861, found many more believing that it was the time.

SLAVERY: DEMOCRACY AND HYPOCRISY

To the contemporary ear, slavery is an abhorrent word, seeming inconsistent with the progress of civilization. But as we are aware, slavery is still a sad reality, whether literally or symbolically in our world. Moorhead tells us that slavery is steeped in the tradition of society, with historical records supporting this. The rationalization for slavery appears to be the sense that existence had a "natural order."[144] An assigned membership to a hierarchy is present in some form in all cultures. The designation "middle class," for example, is a hierarchical assignment. This sense of natural order is even found in the Bible, which records slavery as not only an established facet of life of the time but demands obedience on the part of the enslaved. The presence of slavery in the Bible certainly served as a handy rationalization for those predisposed to continuing the practice. But those opposed to the practice could find Biblical support in the accounts of the efforts of God and Moses to free an enslaved people. It would be encouraging to note that the decline of slavery in the world followed the rise of Christianity from cult to world religion. However, it is more likely that any diminishment of slavery in the progress of history is more closely linked to its economic viability at a given time.[145]

Slavery lost its institutional grip during the Middle Ages, but the larger issue of its morality went unchallenged. The settlement of the New World, therefore, brought with it the mindset of slavery as an option, an option lacking any formidable opposing philosophical structure.[146]

Protestantism was an import to America, and came to these shores as a work in progress. As we have seen with the American experience ≠ the challenges of the wilderness, encounters with Native Americans, war, the coronation of America as the "new Israel," and the seemingly continual anticipation of the millennium ≠ all helped to change the countenance of Protestantism. Added wrinkles came from the Enlightenment and humanistic thought, as well as the confusion surrounding the Democracy that was taking shape in America, the land of freedom for all but the enslaved.[147]

Neither progressive thought, nor the creation of a new nation did much to stop the flow of slaves into America. In the forty-year period between 1720-1760, history notes that slave ships brought 150,000 Africans to these shores.[148]

Even in the annals of the long human tradition of enslavement, American slavery occupies an unusual niche, and in a variety of ways exceeded that of other, "non-civilized" cultures in both severity and inhumanity. The legal, government sanctioned subjugation of American slaves was astounding. African slaves were denied the right to simple humanity, because legally, they were property. As property, there were no family rights, thus families were divided and members sold at the discretion of the slaveholder. In previous cultures, slaves were accorded full marriage and family privileges.[149]

The destiny of slavery in America was guided by economics. In colonial America, slaves were required in both the North and South, precluding any meaningful anti-slavery activity. Over time and especially after the revolution, the economic climate of the country began to change. The industrialization of the North rendered slavery a discardable economic option. In 1776, Adam Smith's treatise *The Wealth of Nations* sounded a death knell to slavery in the North, depicting the slave system as economically inefficient.[150] In the South, with its deeply imbedded agrarianism, slavery was essential. So powerful was the economic pull of slavery, that it split churches into Northern and Southern factions. Those Southern churches that spoke out against slavery did so at the risk of losing membership to other congregations.[151]

SLAVES AND THE MILLENNIUM

In addition to losing their freedom, families, and humanity, Africans in America also needed to face the dissolution of their religious tradition. The practice of collecting and selling slaves disintegrated tribes, as the members of each tribe were separated and sold throughout their captive land. Subsequently, members of different tribes were forced together. For some time, slaves who chose or were allowed to do so, practiced their common rite and ritual.[152]

In the enthusiasm to convert *all* to Christianity in preparation for the millennium, the seventeenth century faithful pondered the question of whether African slaves should be included. After all, it was determined, Native Americans were being converted. But there was much resistance to the idea, because of concerns that being saved might somehow threaten ownership, or presage vengeance on the part of slaves, and thereby lead to equality with whites.[153]

The Great Awakening of the eighteenth century settled the issue. Preaching, the primary medium of the day, became widespread. Among the Baptists, lay preaching was encouraged so that as many as possible could share in the "feeling of the enthusiasm" that was the hallmark of religious practice of the day. The "openness and expressiveness" of Baptist services touched a familiar chord in the Africans, as a memory from home. The evangelical movement was not, as were other varieties of Protestantism, concerned with social status. Evangelicals did not see the poverty of material possessions as a measurement in God's eyes, as God, they felt, evaluated in spiritual terms. With this view, the mid-eighteenth century found growing numbers of Africans converting to Christianity, and by the end of the eighteenth century ensconced African preachers.[154]

In Christianity, Africans found a way to fill the void that slavery had created in their existence. Christianity provided the anchor of common experience for members of tribes dissolved, a foundation to build a new tradition, to bind a people through the experience of spiritual cohesion.[155]

Previously, we have referred to the work of Barkun, and his insights into the mechanisms involved in steering a people toward a millennial vision. One of the concepts was the *true society*, essentially the core of the identification of an individual or culture. For the profound reasons already illustrated, the true society of the Africans was destroyed, and the groundwork for a vision to accommodate the dire circumstances of a people were laid, and a medium for that, a new religious practice, was adopted.

A facet of the faith of Africans was the singing of spirituals. This practice served a dual purpose. First, it was a connection to God throughout the day, an expression that could be practiced even while working. It represented a kind of "oral meditation." In addition, the singing of spirituals was a cultural expression of Africans as a people of Biblical significance, and of their identity as a people to be freed by God. Thus their millennial vision was created and articulated in the meter of the spiritual, sung in anticipation of the deliverance of a Moses to lead them to their Canaan.[156] The mantle of Moses was assumed by Nat Turner, in 1831. Weary of the prolonged wait for a heavenly deliverance, this self-perceived agent of God assembled seventy fellow slaves in a short-lived revolt.[157] The bloody uprising left many dead, but kindled the anti-slavery movement in the North.

Having been excluded from all else in America, African slaves, and later African-Americans, invested themselves in the institution of Christianity in the form of the black church. Created by African-Americans for themselves, the black church became a haven for trust in the community. Over the years, and to this day, the African-American church community became a primary institute for the nurturing of their people's leadership.[158]

THE BROKEN PROMISE

War, by any measure, is commensurate with horror, but even employing the gauge of previous conflicts, the Civil War emerges as particularly gruesome. Whether because of the passion inherent in brother fighting brother, or the inspiration of a millennial cause, there was a particular viciousness in the battles. Religious observers in the North saw the carnage as more than just the simple conflict of abolition and slavery. Slavery for them became a disease, one that infected every aspect of Southern life, responsible for "immorality, ignorance, and the poverty of the masses."[159] Truly, they felt, this was the source of evil in society, responsible for afflicting the very spirit of society. This pervasive corruption had become the Anti-Christ.[160]

The promise of good once again pervaded the thoughts of Americans with the passage of the *Emancipation Proclamation* on January 1, 1863. Lincoln's declaration stated that all slaves in states in rebellion were declared forever free. The power of this statement persuaded the faithful, in the light of the defeat of the perceived Anti-Christ, to harbor millennial feelings once more. The American promise, as the chosen nation of God, seemed once again ready to be fulfilled. Signs of this were apparent. Moorhead reports that as many as 200,000 battlefield conversions had taken place during the war.[161] By 1864, charities had collected over *$212 million* from the American people to ease the pain of the war.[162] The sacred mission of the war, and its approaching culmination, seemed to be best depicted in *The Battle Hymn of the Republic:* "Mine eyes have seen the glory of the coming of the lord..."

Sean M. O'Shea and Meryl A. Walker

By 1865, the war had ended and Lincoln, who engaged the Anti-Christ of slavery, was dead. In the Reconstruction Era, the promises of an America of peace and justice, where all were truly free, seemed empty and broken. The grip of millennial thought had evidently not included a preparation for peace. The Golden Age that was to follow became a Gilded Age, where a scratch to the surface revealed the dark immorality of men.[163] What would remain, and would carry into the next century, was the American sense of a divine imprimatur on their destiny. Further challenges would lie in wait as the twentieth century approached, and the nation headed into a troubling vortex of events, including the threat of technologies that could summon the Apocalypse.

Chapter Five Bibliography

1. Robertson, J.O. (1980). *American Myth/American Reality.* (p. 33). New York: Hill and Wang. As cited in: May, R. (1991). *The Cry for Myth.* (p. 46). New York: Delta Books.
2. May, R. (1991). *The Cry for Myth.* (p. 91). New York: Delta Books.
3. *Ibid.,* (p. 91-92).
4. Campbell, J. (1972) *Myths to Live by.* (p. 2). New York: Viking Books.
5. *Ibid.*
6. *Ibid.*
7. *Ibid.,* (p.2-3).
8. *Ibid.,* (p. 3).
9. May, R. (1991). *The Cry for Myth.* (p. 92). New York: Delta Books.
10. Renaissance. *Microsoft Encarta Encyclopedia* (1996).
11. May, R. (1991). *The Cry for Myth.* (p. 92). New York: Delta Books.
12. Renaissance. *Microsoft Encarta Encyclopedia* (1996).
13. Campbell, J. (1972) *Myths to Live by.* (p. 4). New York: Viking Books.
14. May, R. (1991). *The Cry for Myth.* (p. 92). New York: Delta Books.
15. *Ibid.*
16. Eliade, M. (1985). *A History of Religious Ideas: From Muhammad to the Age of Reforms* (p. 237). Chicago: University of Chicago Press.
17. Kappler, C. Monstres, *Demons et Merveilles `a la fin du Moyen Age.* (p. 108). As cited in Eliade, M. (1985). *A History of Religious Ideas: From Muhammad to the Age of Reforms* (p. 237). Chicago: University of Chicago Press.
18. Cotterell, A. (1986). *A Dictionary of World Mythology.* (p. 195-197). New York: Oxford University Press.
19. *Ibid.*

20. Hopfe, L.M. (1994). *Religions of the World.* (p. 34). New York: Macmillan College Publishing Company.

21. Campbell, J. (1969). *Primitive Mythology.* (p. 208-210). New York: Penguin Books.

22. *Ibid.,* (p. 146).

23. *Ibid.,* (p. 147).

24. *Ibid.,* (p. 148).

25. Eliade, M. (1954). *The Myth of the Eternal Return.* (p. 14). Princeton: Princeton University Press.

26. Hopfe, L.M. (1994). *Religions of the World.* (p. 34). New York: Macmillan College Publishing Company.

27. *Ibid.*

28. *Ibid.*

29. *Ibid.*

30. *Ibid.,* (p. 40-41).

31. *Ibid.,* (p. 40).

32. *Ibid.,* (p. 41).

33. Eliot, A. (1976). *The Universal Myths.* (p. 29-30). New York: Meridian Books.

34. *Ibid.,* (p. 28).

35. Hopfe, L.M. (1994). *Religions of the World.* (p. 45). New York: Macmillan College Publishing Company.

36. *Ibid.*

37. *Ibid.*

38. *Ibid.*

39. *Ibid.*

40. *Ibid.,* (p. 46).

41. *Ibid.*

42. Eliade, M. (1985). *A History of Religious Ideas: From Muhammad to the Age of Reforms.* (p. 88). Chicago: University of Chicago Press.

43. Jordan, M. (1995). *Myths of the World: a Thematic Encyclopedia.* (p. 107). London: Kyle Cathie Limited.

44. Eliot, A. (1976). *The Universal Myths.* (p. 270). New York: Meridian Books.

45. *Ibid.,* (p. 78).

46. *Ibid.*

47. *Ibid.,* (p.79-80)

48. *Ibid.*

49. Leeming, D. A. (1990). *The World of Myth: an Anthology.* (p. 84). New York: Oxford University Press.

50. *Ibid.*

51. *Ibid.*

52. *Ibid.*

53. Eliade, M. (1954). *The Myth of the Eternal Return.* (p. 88). Princeton: Princeton University Press.

54. Armstrong, K. (1993). *A History of God.* (p.279). New York: Ballantine Books.

55. *Ibid.,* (p. 281).

56. *Ibid.*

57. *Ibid.*

58. *Ibid.,* (p. 283).

59. *Ibid.*

60. *Ibid.,* (p. 283-284).

61. *Ibid.*

62. Helmert, A. and Delbanco, A., Editors. (1985) *The Puritans in America: a Narrative Anthology.* (p. 1). Cambridge: Harvard University Press.

63. *Ibid.*

64. *Ibid.,* (p. 2).

65. *Ibid.,* (p. 3).

66. *Ibid.*

67. *Ibid.,* (p. 4).

68. *Ibid.,* (p. 7).

69. *Ibid.,* (p. 8).

70. *Ibid.,* (p. 9).

71. *Ibid.,* (p.7).

72. Barkun, M. (1986). *Disaster and the Millennium.* (p. 82). Syracuse: Syracuse University Press.

73. *Ibid.*

74. *Ibid.,* (p. 24).

75. *Ibid.,* (p. 84).

76. Dudley, W. and O'Neill, T., Editors. (1994). *Puritanism: Opposing Viewpoints.* (p. 265). San Diego: Greenhaven Press.

77. Lovejoy, D. (1985). *Religious Enthusiasm in the New World: Heresy to Revolution.* (p. 17).Cambridge: Harvard University Press.

78. Maclear, J. (1975). *Puritanism and the End of the World.* In Dudley, W. and O'Neill, T., Editors. (1994). Puritanism: Opposing Viewpoints. (p. 265). San Diego: Greenhaven Press.

79. Lovejoy, D. (1985). *Religious Enthusiasm in the New World: Heresy to Revolution.* (p. 12). Cambridge: Harvard University Press.

80. *Ibid.,* (p. 12-13).

81. Helmert, A. and Delbanco, A., Editors. (1985) *The Puritans in America: a Narrative Anthology.* (p. 10-11). Cambridge: Harvard University Press.

82. *Ibid.,* (p. 291).

83. Lovejoy, D. (1985). *Religious Enthusiasm in the New World: Heresy to Revolution.* (p. 17-18). Cambridge: Harvard University Press.

84. Dudley, W. and O'Neill, T., Editors. (1994). *Puritanism: Opposing Viewpoints.* (p. 9-10). San Diego: Greenhaven Press.

85. *Ibid.,* (p. 15).

86. *Ibid.*

87. *Ibid.*

88. *Ibid.,* (p. 88).

89. Helmert, A. and Delbanco, A., Editors. (1985) *The Puritans in America: a Narrative Anthology.* (p. 8). Cambridge: Harvard University Press.

90. Armstrong, K. (1993). *A History of God.* (p.279). New York: Ballantine Books.

91. Ibid.

92. Marty, M. E., (1984). *Pilgrims in Their Own Lands.* (p. 132). Boston: Little, Brown and Company.

93. Lovejoy, D. (1985). *Religious Enthusiasm in the New World: Heresy to Revolution.* (p. 178-179). Cambridge: Harvard University Press

94. *Ibid.,* (p. 179).

95. *Ibid.*

96. Marsden, G. M. (1990). *Religion and American Culture.* (p. 31). New York: Harcourt, Brace, Jovanovich.

97. Bloom, H. (1992). *The American Religion: the Emergence of the Post-Christian Nation.* (p.269). New York: Simon and Schuster.

98. Marsden, G. M. (1990). *Religion and American Culture.* (p. 24). New York: Harcourt, Brace, Jovanovich.

99. Lovejoy, D. (1985). *Religious Enthusiasm in the New World: Heresy to Revolution.* (p. 179). Cambridge: Harvard University Press.

100. Bloom, H. (1992). *The American Religion: the Emergence of the Post- Christian Nation.* (p. 269). New York: Simon and Schuster.

101. Marsden, G. M. (1990). *Religion and American Culture.* (p. 40). New York: Harcourt, Brace, Jovanovich.

102. Lovejoy, D. (1985). *Religious Enthusiasm in the New World: Heresy to Revolution.* (p. 246). Cambridge: Harvard University Press.

103. Marsden, G. M. (1990). *Religion and American Culture.* (p. 29). New York: Harcourt, Brace, Jovanovich.

104. *Ibid.*

105. *Ibid.,* (p. 27).

106. *Ibid.,* (p. 40).

107. Lovejoy, D. (1985). *Religious Enthusiasm in the New World: Heresy to Revolution.* (p. 215). Cambridge: Harvard University Press.

108. Marsden, G. M. (1990). *Religion and American Culture.* (p. 40). New York: Harcourt, Brace, Jovanovich.

109. Marty, M. E., (1984). *Pilgrims in Their Own Lands.* (p. 134). Boston: Little, Brown and Company.

110. Marsden, G. M. (1990). *Religion and American Culture.* (p. 40). New York: Harcourt, Brace, Jovanovich.

111. Lovejoy, D. (1985). *Religious Enthusiasm in the New World:*

Heresy to Revolution. (p. 226). Cambridge: Harvard University Press.

112. Marini, S.A. (1982).*Radical Sects of Revolutionary New England.* (p. 173). Cambridge: Harvard University Press.

113. *Ibid.,* (p. 46).

114. *Ibid.,* (p. 47).

115. *Ibid.*

116. Morse, F. (1980). *The Shakers and the World's People.* (p. 22). Hanover: The University Press of New England.

117. Marini, S.A. (1982). *Radical Sects of Revolutionary New England.* (p. 47). Cambridge: Harvard University Press.

118. *Ibid.*

119. *Ibid.,* (p. 5).

120. *Ibid.,* (p. 5).

121. Barkun, M. (1986). *Disaster and the Millennium.* (p. 21). Syracuse: Syracuse University Press.

122. *Ibid.,* (p. 23).

123. Lovejoy, D. (1985). *Religious Enthusiasm in the New World: Heresy to Revolution.* (p. 226). Cambridge: Harvard University Press.

124. *Ibid.*

125. Barkun, M. (1986). *Disaster and the Millennium.* (p. 23). Syracuse: Syracuse University Press.

126. Moorhead, J. (1978). *American Apocalypse: Yankee Protestants and the Civil War 1860-1869.* (p. 5). New Haven: Yale University Press.

127. Doan, R. A. (1987). *The Miller Heresy, Millennialism, and American Culture.* (p. 12). Philadelphia: Temple University Press.

128. *Ibid.,* (p. 16).

129. *Ibid.,* (p. 18).

130. *Ibid.,* (p. 19).

131. Marsden, G. M. (1990). *Religion and American Culture.* (p. 80). New York: Harcourt, Brace, Jovanovich.

132. Numbers, R. L., and Numbers, J. S. (1985). "Millerism and

Madness: a Study of 'Religious Insanity' in Nineteenth Century America." *Bulletin of the Menninger Clinic,* 49 (4), 289-320.

133. Marsden, G. M. (1990). *Religion and American Culture.* (p. 80). New York: Harcourt, Brace, Jovanovich.

134. Marty, M. E., (1984). *Pilgrims in Their Own Lands.* (p. 322). Boston: Little, Brown and Company.

135. *Ibid.,* (p. 190).

136. Moorhead, J. (1978). *American Apocalypse: Yankee Protestants and the Civil War 1860- 1869* (p. 56-57). New Haven: Yale University Press.

137. *Ibid.,* (p. 57).

138. *Ibid.,* (p. 58-59)

139. *Ibid.,* (p. 61).

140. *Ibid.,* (p. 11).

141. *Ibid.,* (p. 13).

142. *Ibid.,* (p. 19-20).

143. *Ibid.,* (p. 11).

144. *Ibid.,* (p. 83).

145. *Ibid.,* (p. 83).

146. *Ibid.*

147. *Ibid.*

148. Marty, M. E., (1984). *Pilgrims in Their Own Lands.* (p. 228). Boston: Little,Brown and Company.

149. Marsden, G. M. (1990). *Religion and American Culture.* (p. 64). New York: Harcourt, Brace, Jovanovich.

150. Moorhead, J. (1978). *American Apocalypse: Yankee Protestants and the Civil War 1860- 1869* (p. 84). New Haven: Yale University Press.

151. Marty, M. E., (1984). *Pilgrims in Their Own Lands.* (p. 243). Boston: Little, Brown and Company.

152. Marsden, G. M. (1990). *Religion and American Culture.* (p. 67). New York: Harcourt, Brace, Jovanovich.

153. Lovejoy, D. (1985). *Religious Enthusiasm in the New World: Heresy to Revolution.* (p. 197-198). Cambridge: Harvard University Press.

154. Marsden, G. M. (1990). *Religion and American Culture.* (p. 67). New York: Harcourt, Brace, Jovanovich.

155. *Ibid.,* (p. 68).

156. *Ibid.,* (p. 68-69)

157. Marty, M. E., (1984). *Pilgrims in Their Own Lands.* (p. 239). Boston: Little,Brown and Company.

158. Marsden, G. M. (1990). *Religion and American Culture.* (p. 69). New York: Harcourt, Brace, Jovanovich.

159. Moorhead, J. (1978). *American Apocalypse: Yankee Protestants and the Civil War 1860- 1869* (p. 111). New Haven: Yale University Press.

160. *Ibid.*

161. *Ibid.,* (p. 70).

162. *Ibid.,* (p. 68).

163. Marsden, G. M. (1990). *Religion and American Culture.* (p. 99). New York: Harcourt, Brace, Jovanovich.

Chapter Six

The Millennium in Contemporary America

"Our society, like a battered and abused child, is fearful and inse-cure. The almighty technology of our post-industrial age seemingly has made machines and their allied military weapons our cruel mas-ters. Society responds as if it wants to return to the warm security of the womb."[1]

FIN DE SIECLE

The end of the nineteenth century produced scattered reports of what has been called "fin de siecle (end of the century) mad-ness."[2] One observer of the era described this state as one in which "...grim humor, a feeling of impending doom, and an odd con-fusion of hectic restlessness"[3] were present. Others were more opti-mistic. Anyone taking inventory of the technological achievements of the nineteenth century could not help but be impressed. Railways crossed the country, steamboats littered the waterways, and the telephone appeared, an instrument that seemed to eliminate the dis-tance between conversing parties. And if one were to add to this already impressive list the miracles of photography, electricity, and antiseptics,[4] to an observer of the era, the nineteenth century was a glorious time serving as a mere precursor to the promise of the twentieth century. The promise was such that some "...were led to hope that progress might even bring some thought undreamed of, some new and happier guess at the great central truth which forev-er allures and forever eludes our grasp."[5]

One hundred years later, at the threshold of another *fin de siecle*, we can understand and appreciate the cares and hopes of nine-teenth century America. The technological promise that our turn of the century ancestors anticipated for the twentieth century has sur-passed the boundaries of their imaginations. Arthur C. Clarke has often alluded to the fact that it is hard for us to appreciate how rapidly technology has advanced, because we exist in the midst of the progression.[6] The following illustration will provide an alternative perspective:

Let us create a fictional character, a woman, who will be gifted with a long life. And, because we are on the eve of the millennium, we will call her Eve. Eve was born in 1903, and, for the sake of our illustration, has recently celebrated her ninety-fourth birthday.

In the year that Eve was born, 1903, two bicycle repairmen, Orville and Wilbur Wright, made the first powered air flight, which lasted *twelve seconds*. This accomplishment was a mere hobby for the brothers, who didn't even bother to tell anyone about it at first. In 1906, when Eve was three, Europeans were exploring the military applications of the airplane. By 1917, when Eve was fourteen, airplanes had seen limited combat duty in World War I. By the time of her twenty-third birthday, in 1926, Eve could read about Dr. Robert Goddard's first rocket. The following year, Charles Lindbergh flew across the Atlantic. In less than a quarter century, manned flight progressed from twelve seconds to thirty-three and one half hours; from one hundred twenty feet to three thousand, six hundred and thirty miles.

As Eve's life progressed, so did man's movement in the air. When she was forty-four, Eve saw reports about a "rocket plane" that traveled faster than sound, 740 miles per hour. Ten years later, when a Soviet rocket placed a man-made object into space, Eve was not yet fifty-five. In her life thus far, man has progressed from being barely able to raise a modified glider from a beach in North Carolina, to propelling an object into space. Over the next few years, Eve reads and witnesses through television the exploits of dogs, monkeys, and finally, man after man, as they are launched into space. By the time she was sixty-six, men have walked on the moon. In the years to follow, more men would reach the moon, women would finally take their place among astronauts, and space shuttles would make ventures outside of this world so routinely that people hardly attend to the news of the flights anymore. By the time she reached her venerable eighties, Eve was watching reports about exploratory satellites to the outer planets and the space station orbiting the earth. At 94, Eve saw the televised pictures of Sojourner on Mars. How was it possible that in a lifetime, albeit a long one, so much progress could have been made? With technology moving at such a mind-numbing rate, what could the future hold?

The scenario of flight was selected as an easy example. Any number of other variables could have illustrated the phenomenal rate of technological progress equally well. The progress of communications, starting with print and culminating in fiber optical and cellular technology, was another option, as was the evolution of medical research that finds itself on the ethically precarious precipice of cloning.

But as we bask in the glow of our awesome breakthroughs in all fields and recognize the exponential gains made over our nineteenth century forebears, we also are aware that their grimness, fear of impending doom, and confusion have also expanded exponentially within us. The alluring and elusive truth sought in the past and hoped for in the present has still, sadly, been evasive. The only difference for us, as we conclude the twentieth century, is that our cry for the comfort of that central truth is more urgent, and more despondent.

THE BURDEN OF OMNISCIENCE

The Spanish-American War, which began in 1898, may be familiar to us because it was during this war that the term *yellow journalism* was coined. Yellow journalism describes the sensationalist tactics employed by Joseph Pulitzer and his newspaper, the *New York World,* and William Randolf Hearst and his newspaper, the *New York Journal.*[7] These media giants of the day exerted powerful influence over the citizens who were following their coverage of the war and related events. The birth of a new century would also mark the origins of what we now call "the media;" ostensibly the recorders of events, but at times, the creators of events as well.

The year 1900 saw the introduction of the "box" camera, which made the almost one hundred year old process of photography accessible to all. The ease and portability of the camera, combined with the established medium of news, were the recipe for a new medium called *photojournalism*, which would be produced in news magazines.[8] Mental images of the news no longer had to be created. The reality of an event could now be depicted as it actually occurred. The reporting of an event *during* its actual occurrence would soon become a possibility as well. In 1901, Marconi transmitted radio signals across the Atlantic Ocean for the first time, using a device that strengthened the signal. The device was called an antenna, because it looked like the appendage on an insect's head.[9]

During this period, we can also chart the rise of the crucial medium called *flickers*. Near the end of the previous century, Thomas Edison had built the first studio for producing flickers, or moving pictures. Despite his attempts to monopolize the infant medium, others succeeded in starting their own successful ventures. Some went to a "backwater suburb" of Los Angeles called Hollywood to set up shop.[10] Motion pictures, or "movies," are so much more than entertainment or an information vehicle. Film is the contemporary medium of myth. Who we are or want to be, as well as what we loathe or desire, are projected on that screen. Certainly, the machine in the back of the theater is not the only projector at work. A further indicator of the importance of film and film personalities in our culture is the fact that a number of our political leaders have come from the industry.[11] One, Ronald Reagan, was President of the United States for eight years.

There are many other "media events" that are part of the development of this century. Two others will be mentioned briefly: the first is the first television transmission in 1933, and the second is the invention of the transistor in 1948.[12] The importance of the invention of television needs no discussion. The invention of the transistor is important because bulky and heavy electronic equipment underwent a metamorphosis to small, light, transportable devices. We are admitting our age when we can remember when the latest gadget that one *had to have* was a transistor radio.

One view of the history of this century, then, is that it is a chronicle of the gradual immersion of the individual in media of all types. Media are available at work. Media are available at home. Media are available during the commute from home to work. Media are always available. There is a very positive aspect to this immersion, in that becoming an informed individual is no longer a *pursuit*, because there is nothing to pursue. Whatever is needed (or not needed) is at our fingertips. In his *Protean Self: Human Resilience in a Fragmented Age*,[13] Robert Jay Lifton discusses Marshall McLuhan's noted 1960s concept of the "global village." The global village was seen as the world, metaphorically reduced in size through the establishment of a "single communications network."[14] Perhaps McLuhan has, in addition to his other talents, shown himself to be a prophet. The single communications network, combining television/ internet/ computer, is slated for early next century. Regardless, McLuhan's assertion that the media were creating an environment of "instant aware-ness"[15] has been present for some time. In the infancy of television, there was a program hosted by legendary newsman Edward R. Murrow called *You Are There*. The premise of the program was to combine the insightful commentary of the host with film footage of important occurrences, to make the viewer a veritable witness to the event. The contemporary omnipresence of electronic media has made that premise an actuality. One will recall the Gulf War, and the intense television coverage it received. We watched as missiles struck their targets, and witnessed a war in much the same way as an entertainment event. Today, for whatever is deemed newsworthy, we *are* there, *everywhere, always*.

There are, however, some difficulties with continual, instant awareness. Lifton, in his writings, has said much about the informa-tion that flies at the individual from "media saturation." We are, he states, victims of "bombardment."[16] From this bombardment comes our burden of omniscience, as we are held captive to the events of the world, aware that the business of news is so much more often than not the delivery and depiction of someone's pain, a pain we are incapable of assuaging.

Our life experience has taught us that repeated exposure to a stimulus results in an experience called *learning*. The completion of learning is *mastery*, which is an indicator that information has become an accepted part of our experiential repertoire. We also know that repeated exposure to a stimulus can result in *desensitiza-tion*, which is a diminished reaction of the senses to a stimulus that previously generated a powerful reaction. A useful example of the above is the therapy used for phobic patients, called *increased desensitization*. A claustrophobe, for example, anticipates a calami-ty when confined to a space from which he/she perceives no exit. Sweating, heart palpitations, and finally panic sweep over the indi-vidual when confined. Through the therapy of increased desensiti-zation, the individual experiences gradually increasing periods of time in confinement until the adverse reaction disappears. The indi-vidual learns, then masters, the fact that there is nothing to fear from confinement. The individual becomes *desensitized* to the adverse experience. He/she has learned to diminish their reaction, to minimize their feeling. Media bombardment has created in us a similar desensitization. The horror of murder and the atrocity of child abuse have lost much of their power to generate in us a reaction commensurate with their evil. Lifton refers to this as "psychic numbing."[17]

PSYCHIC APOCALYPSE

"A faulty picture of the world is constantly being so shaken by reality that he feels threatened from many sides."[18] In this opening line, Alfred Adler begins his presentation of the *exclusion tendency*, as well as a textbook description of our contemporary actuality. The *exclusion tendency* is a defense mechanism in reaction to the shock of impending and threatening problems that are a picture of the world,[19] pictures that are inescapable because of media bombardment. In reaction, a person's problems of life are excluded, "shoved aside," in order to "safeguard his picture of the world."[20] In the late twentieth century, the variables that one may need to be excluded are, sorrowfully, multiple. Lifton has examined these variables in his writings much more expansively than is possible here, but their mention is required in order to consider the apocalyptic issues that confront us in fin de siecle America.

The end of World War II forced the world to confront the unspeakable abomination of genocide. The world needed to contend with the fact that a nation with an established Christian tradition not only premeditated, but systematically planned, mass murder. A government actually established the procedures and created the facilities whose sole purpose was to terminate not only Jewish men, women, and children, but *anyone* determined to be unfit to live, which included the physically or mentally disabled and homosexuals. This plan was so heinous that it included an initiative to import additional Jews, so that they too, could be eliminated.[21]

The Nuremburg Trials were conducted following the war in an effort to recoup some semblance of justice in order to show that the world community would not tolerate such horrors. For decades, Simon Wiesenthal would comb the world tracking down war criminals in an effort to communicate that there was to be no hiding place from justice. Clearly, no people would be victim, nor the world an idle witness, to such a crime ever again.

Needless to say, some ultimately evil threshold was crossed, because the media would continue, over the last half of this century, to bombard us with images of genocide in Cambodia, Rwanda, and Bosnia, as well as Stalin's death march. Television and news magazines provided us immediately with the gruesome evidence. And still it happened. Our exclusion tendencies kicked in, our psychic numbness became operational, our horror of death became desensitized. But somewhere within us, we are *psychically wounded*.

As if genocide wasn't enough to contend with, the Second World War produced atomic energy; the technological capability for mass destruction that quickly evolved into the more potent development of nuclear energy. This capability produced the capacity for instant genocide, as exemplified by the destruction of Nagasaki and Hiroshima, as well as the psychological cloud of world destruction that still hangs over us one half century later. The arms race that followed World War II, called the Cold War, took its psychic toll and presented to us the reality of our own extinction. These writers clearly recall the frightening impact that the 1962 Cuban Missile Crisis had upon their consciousness, even when only ten years old. In a nationally televised address, President Kennedy backed Soviet leader Nikita Khrushchev into a political corner. Khrushchev was presented with two options: to withdraw missiles from Cuba or go to war, with nuclear implications. The fate of the world hung in the balance for four interminable days until Khrushchev backed down.

In 1981, the American Psychiatric Association conducted a study of the psychological impact of the nuclear threat on children and adolescents. The results of the study, which included 4000 Boston area students, showed that the nuclear threat "had penetrated deeply into their consciousness."[22] Respondents indicated feelings of fear, helplessness, cynicism, and bitterness; they stated their skepticism about their futures, and the wisdom of making long term plans.[23] Perhaps there is no hopelessness that can rival the denial of a future. In his studies, Lifton has labeled this "nuclear numbing."[24]

The events transpiring in the conclusion of this century have not ceased to introduce additional hazards to our existence. Nuclear energy, even when purportedly utilized for mankind's benefit, has not been without hazard. In 1979, a "nuclear incident" occurred at the Three Mile Island Plant near Harrisburg, Pennsylvania. An environmentally disastrous core meltdown was avoided that threatened the lives of *millions*.[25] In 1986, the outcome was not so fortunate for the citizens of the Soviet Union. At the nuclear power plant in

Chernobyl, eighty miles north of Kiev, the third most populous city in Russia, one of the nuclear reactors "went out of control." Reports of the incident are not extensive, given the secrecy of the Soviet regime at the time, but what is known is that there is ample evidence, some of which has been seen on television, of the radioactive devastation inflicted on the people unfortunate enough to live in the area. As of 1990, *millions* of people were living on contaminated ground. As of this writing, part of Chernobyl is still operative to meet the electricity needs of the locals.[26]

The assault of Chernobyl on the environment of the Soviet Union and Europe as far east as Great Britain, raises other environmental issues of the late twentieth century. Part of the burden of the omniscience that we are feeling is attributable to the ongoing reports of environmental disaster. The extinction list of species grows continually, forcing us to confront the simple truth of our own fragility, since we see that life is guaranteed to no species on this planet, including our own. Animal rights activists, growing ever more militant and aggressive, rightfully suggest to us that initiatives to protect animals will provide a conscious respect for life that will extend to *us*. Desensitization toward the lives of animals is part of desensitization toward all life, including human life.

In 1989 the *Exxon Valdez*, an oil tanker, spilled 40,000 tons of oil in Prince William Sound, Alaska. The oil spread over 400 miles and covered 1,500 miles of coastline. The devastation continued for weeks after the incident, as the oil-water mix found its way into fishing and wildlife areas. Despite recovery efforts, only fifteen percent of the oil was actually removed from the ocean. More frighteningly, this disaster represented only twenty percent of the cargo; the other eighty percent was successfully pumped onto another vessel. Over 600,000 seabirds were killed in the devastation, with *six billion dollars* in other damage reported. In 1996, seven years later, oil residue could still be found on the Alaskan beaches.[27]

The damage that is being perpetrated on the environment has been seen in more ways than one. The Central and South American rain forest has been another environmental area of concern. The burning of this forest, or its denuding for lumber at the rate of many acres per day implies the extinction of species of animals and plants, some of which are yet unknown, as well as the people indigenous to the area, who know no other way of existence. As if that were not tragedy enough, other repercussions of rainforest destruction have been suggested. Global warming is believed to be augmented by rainforest destruction, since the world's rainforests account for most of the transformation of carbon dioxide into oxygen. The less rainforests, the more carbon dioxide, and thus the warmer the earth will become. The 1992 movie *Medicine Man* has suggested that the preservation of the rainforest could result in miraculous medicinal benefits to mankind; this story is not so incredible when one considers that many of our modern synthetic medicines are based on compounds originally extracted from plants.

Another threat to our existence comes from sources that are not readily seen. The plentitude of life on earth includes the microscopic world. Another fin de siecle concern is what sort of beings, if any, might exist on other planets. One scientist has cautioned that our first encounter may very well be with a microbe. His rationale was that seventy percent of life on this world is microscopic, so the same might be the case elsewhere. Day to day, microbes are extremely beneficial to the wellbeing of our planet, even if we just consider their cyclical role in decomposing dead material into matter that will nurture the life that is to follow.

However, we are also well aware of the threat that microscopic life poses to us. We have covered the devastation of the Black Death, an affliction that eliminated one third of the world in the Middle Ages. Early in this century, influenza claimed as many as twenty million victims.[28] Before the inception of powerful antibiotics, death from pneumonia was a common occurrence. And when these writers were children, the crippling disease polio ravaged the 1950's.

Newer and more frightening microbes have found their way into our world. It has been suggested that the presence of these killers is related to our invasion of forests and jungles throughout the world. One new disease is AIDS, attributed to an infection received from an African forest monkey. Infections of this disease have been recorded as far back as 1968, but worldwide attention began with its first characterization in 1981. Since this disease was first found in the homosexual community, it was tragically ignored for sadly discriminatory and ultimately unforgivable reasons. The connection between AIDS and sex, especially homosexual sex, made this disease a particularly difficult issue in the conservative administration of President Reagan.

Originally one hundred percent fatal, AIDS claimed over 315,000 dead by 1993 in America alone.[29] Recently there has been some semblance of hope for victims of the disease, as a "cocktail" of drugs has given a new revitalization to *some*. At this writing there is still no cure. The disease continues to devastate those without access to the full regimen of drugs. Worldwide, the effects of AIDS are increasing exponentially. The shock of AIDS has ravaged Southeast Asia and Africa. Some reports from Africa state that in some villages an entire generation of adults has been taken by the disease, meaning that an entire generation of children have lost their parents. The threat of AIDS has been harrowing for its life taking toll, but also because of how it is most often transmitted; via sex, which is commensurate with life. Whether it is the vehicle to the creation of life, or the celebration of life and love, it has been psychically devastating to contend with the fact that this instinctual ecstasy could possibly bear the threat of death.

There have been a variety of reports in recent years regarding the peril of the Ebola virus. The first outbreaks of the virus occurred in 1976, in Zaire, Africa. The source of the Ebola infection appears to be monkeys, some of which have been captured and sold throughout the world as pets or research animals. At an outbreak in Zaire in 1976, 340 people died. Twenty years later, outbreaks of this virus continue, with another outbreak in Zaire in 1996 killing 245, and yet another in Gabon in the same year, killing 13.[30] The mortality rate for infected victims is about eighty percent. Infection is believed to be caused by contact with the bodily secretions of carriers. In Africa, human infection is caused by the consumption of monkey meat, an important source of protein for the impoverished.

Ebola has appeared twice in the United States, in Reston, Virginia in 1989, and in Alice, Texas in 1996. The forms of the virus in these circumstances were lethal to the monkeys in the laboratories, but not to humans. The distributor of the monkeys, located in the Phillippines, was only supposed to supply monkeys raised in captivity; however, wild infected monkeys were somehow included in shipments.[31] Chillingly, experiments have shown that monkeys can develop respiratory infections containing the infectious virus when Ebola is "aerosolized"- *airborne*.[32] There is a definitive human role played in the Ebola threat. Researchers say that overpopulation and poverty are important players in the ongoing menace of this virus.[33]

A final issue to mention in our psychic apocalypse is terrorism. This murderous act of destructive vengeance by one religious or political group against another has become a sadly familiar part of our media bombardment. For residents of the United States, terrorism has mostly been experienced as a news report. The seemingly eternal strife between Israelis and Palestinians, or the events in Northern Ireland, were viewed from a comfortable distance. The World Trade Center bombing, the Olympic Park bombing in Atlanta, and the Oklahoma City bombing have brought the reprehensible act of terrorism home. While the World Trade Center bombing allowed us to direct our outrage at foreign influences, both the Olympic Park bombing and the Oklahoma City bombing, which were far more deadly, appear to have been committed by Americans. Both of these tragedies occurred without warning, victimizing innocent people occupied with the simple task of living.

Fin de siecle America has taught us that in life, there is no safe haven. Our very existence hangs in the balance, and the scale is weighted by the burden of nuclear, biological, environmental, and terrorist perils, constantly illustrated for us through the media. In the face of these assaults to our "true society," many people are seeking, in this time of psychic apocalypse, a new myth to accommodate new realities. Freud said, "People demand illusion, they constantly give what is unreal precedence over what is real."[34] Ernest Becker adds, "The reason why, is that the world is simply too terrible to admit; it tells man that he is a small trembling animal who will decay and die. Illusion changes all this, makes man seem important, vital to the universe, immortal in some way...The masses look to the leaders to give them just the untruth that they need."[35]

CONTEMPORARY MILLENNARIANISM: CULTS

"Man is in constant conflict with his civilization which denies him spontaneous, integral gratification, but this desire although repressed remains in the unconscious and is at the root of Edenic and paradisiacal thinking."[36] This conflict with civilization has been, in recent years, a well reported resistance to established societal institutions, seen by many to be in dramatic decline. The government has been perceived as unnecessarily invasive into the daily lives of its citizens. The government is sullenly accused of imposing countless laws, regulations, and excessive taxes used to fund international pursuits, while ignoring the internal national crises of poverty and illiteracy. Even the established religious institutions seem to be preoccupied with their regulations and demands for mass adherence to behavioral norms.[37] The contemporary media reports of the fall from grace of preachers and priests involved in troublesome sexual activity have augmented this skepticism.

The institution of the family has also been deeply troubled. Under assault from a variety of sociological and economic forces, the family, whatever form it may take, is also frequently in dilemma. The idea of a family as the independent entity that provides for all the needs of its members has disappeared under the pressure of a civilization that simply cannot absorb all of the changes being forced upon it.[38] Even the most basic needs of food, housing, and the provision of sexual information has been assigned to a myriad of agencies, both private and public. Children, then, are learning very early on that answers to their needs can be found outside the home. The issue of basic needs recalls the work of Maslow, who itemized basic needs to include the physiological; security; love and the feeling of belonging; and self-esteem.[39] For the rich or poor denied these basics, an avenue will be pursued that can provide some semblance of need fulfillment. Their sense of alienation, lack of identity, or crisis will propel them. This pursuit may draw individuals to gangs, political movements, satanic groups, or cults.[39]

In the media, the word *cult* has become laden with pejorative meaning. Cult has been recently defined as a fringe group that practices whatever might be at odds with the societal mainstream. It originally stood for the practice of worship within an established religious tradition.[40] If, for example, a group of Roman Catholics practiced a veneration for a particular saint because of that saint's prominent works, they were dubbed a cult. It would be hard to imagine any derisive commentary toward those choosing to follow the path of Mother Theresa as a memorial to her. The focus of her order, attending to the "impoverished of the impoverished," is commensurate with the original meaning of cult. Further, it might serve well that we remember that in the time of John of Patmos, Christianity was considered a cult.

The variability of cults has resulted in a correspondingly inconstant perception of their benefit to their members. One view, the less familiar, is that cults provide positive assistance to its adherents. The remarks of some psychologists, psychiatrists, and sociologists indicate that cults have performed a service that no other established institution can, by providing the means for individuals to contend with and master their drug and alcohol addictions. In addition, cults have been seen to "introduce into the lives of their members, intellectual security, emotional stability, and organized behavioral patterns that contrast sharply with their previously confused and chaotic existence."[41]

The more prevalent view of cults is negative. They are seen as "dangerous institutions that cause severe mental and emotional harm to those who commit themselves to their creeds and lifestyles."[42] Deceit, indoctrination, and mind control are seen as the methods used to ruin members. Charismatic leaders, often self-portrayed as a prophet, or even a god, are dictatorial and exploitative of those purportedly in their care.[43]

Whatever the intent of cults, the indisputable fact is that people, in ever increasing numbers, are drawn to them to fulfill internal cravings that the established society has failed to meet. Among these cravings, *family and community* rank highest. One idea of the construction of family and community is the *commune*.

The commune, in America, has tradition. A notable example is that of the Shakers, founded by Ann Lee. Called "Mother Ann" by her followers, she established a faith carried out in nineteen "societies," which were at first suspect, but finally respected as the "United Society of Believers in Christ's Second Appearing."[44] The respect for this "cult" resulted from the fact that "Shakertowns" were devoid of poverty, crime, and jails. Men and women were equals. In addition to those lofty aspirations, there were, however, practices among the Shakers that might be deemed more unusual. These included the separation of men and women, the abstinence from sex, and their shaking movements during worship, which provided their name.[45] More importantly, and not uncommonly for a communal movement, the Shakers had a millennial character. Ann Lee, the "mother" of the movement, reputed herself to be the Second Coming of Christ. God had determined, she said, that Christ's new revelation would be female.[46,47]

Even for the totally disenfranchised, the step to joining a cult is not a simple one. The failures of the establishment, no matter how deep, are familiar, and part of one's nurturance, and therefore psychologically entrenched. A new commitment to a novel way of viewing existence is terribly risky. The promise of an inventive, non-conventional era, a millennial era, is what is required to make the "leap of faith." The communal effort to accomplish meaningful goals provides the impetus missing in the previous lives of followers. Even the most ordinary of chores in a millennial cult advances the aims of the collective.[48]

An important part of assimilation into the new millennial cult is the crucial factor of *commitment*. Moss-Kanter describes commitment as the "willingness to carry out the requirements of a pattern of social action because he or she sees it as stemming from his or her own basic nature as a person."[49] Commitment to a cult is ultimately an exchange, and the nature of this transaction strongly resembles the commitment made in a relationship. Two people make a commitment to one another in a relationship, whether legally through marriage, or more informally. The benefits of the relationship are clear; the exclusive provision of nurturance, in both material and sexual terms. What is also understood in most of these relationships is that affiliations with others in a nurturing or sexual sense is forbidden. The exchange in a cult is similar, with exclusivity of commitment to the cult thoroughly expected, at the expense of the former societal relationship. The old self is cast off, and a new person is born, sometimes through the processes of coercion and degradation.[50]

The casting off of the old self and the rebirth of a new person within the cult can be accomplished in a variety of ways. The withdrawal from the old world may be literal, through residence in a commune removed from one's former life, which is perceived as inferior or even evil. In addition, inauguration into the life of the movement may require the notion of sacrifice. The privilege of membership in the new society is often purchased at the cost of one's possessions, with the relinquishing of these to the commune seen as the small price of commitment to the new society.[51] With the separation of the individual from their possessions, the transition is still not complete. A new name may be required, sometimes after a ritual. Corresponding to this may be a new "birth" date corresponding to the date of cult membership. Further identification with the movement may be accomplished through a standard mode of dress, and may extend to language and terminology, as well as mannerisms.[52]

Work activity within the cult can be prodigious. Extensive work serves the needs of the day to day survival of the organization, as well as the continuous separation of the member from the outside world and its inhabitants, effectively denying any competition for the grasp of the group. This grasp is also strengthened through the regulation of relationships within the group. Having broken family and friendship ties outside the group, intra-group relations are carefully monitored. Exclusive relations within the group are discouraged, lest the ultimate loyalty to the group as a whole be compromised.[53] Sexual practices are often dealt with in one of two ways. Ann Lee excluded sexual practice among the Shakers. David Koresh, the leader of the Branch Davidians, was reported to have had sexual access to most of the female members of his movement. Alternative ways of expressing sexuality further distance the cult from the established mores of the world from which they seek removal.

Rite and ritual are important to any movement. The meeting of a community and their observance of their "oneness,"[54] further enhances bonding. Moss-Kanter's observation of Durkheim, that religion is the "worship of the immediate social group,"[55] is aptly chosen. For cults, communal gatherings are an affirmation of themselves as an extant and viable entity, surviving and thriving on their own terms. The denigrations cast their way by mainstream society only deepen their resolve. Finally, rite and ritual exercised in communal gatherings provide the platform for reacquaintance with the cosmic forces that are purported to be the guiding reason for the cult's existence. This serves as a reminder of the gift of being chosen, of the specialness sadly absent from their former life, of a link to otherworldly forces, and to a transcendence provided by a leader of seemingly messianic stature.[56]

CONTEMPORARY MESSIAHS

Messiah is a powerful designation. Its meaning, *the Anointed One*, was the Hebrew name for a promised deliverer of man. The Greek translation of the Hebrew Bible presents the word as *Christos*, from which the appellation "Christ" is derived. Christians applied the term to Jesus. In the Hebrew tradition, the messiah is still awaited.[57] Whether in the Hebrew tradition of expectation, or the Christian anticipation of the Second Coming, this long desired deliverer has a substantial group of people longing for His or Her presence. The interminable wait and psychic need, in combination with difficult societal circumstances, have repeatedly caused members of the needy faithful to joyfully designate an "anointed one." None have fulfilled the lofty expectations.

There are many, many historical accounts of people pursuing the throne of messiah. Most reside in the realm of esoterica. A few, such as Ann Lee, are a part of our history. Contemporary America continues to provide us with messianic aspirants. A few of the more media notable are to be briefly presented here.

It has been said that a picture is worth a thousand words. In 1978, pictures circulated the world that depicted the *mass suicide of 913 people*. Kroth, in his study of what is now known as the Jonestown Massacre, reminds us of the fact that mass suicide is an extremely rare occurrence.[58] The Jonestown cult was a microcosm of American society. Kroft tells us that it was a mixture of "senior citizens, whites, blacks, hippies, doctors, middle class executives, orphans, and disadvantaged youth."[59] The leader of this cult was the Reverend Jim Jones, a charismatic preacher to the poor. By 1971, Jones had established "The People's Temple" in San Francisco, attracting followers who perceived him to be the messiah. Reports that he had stolen church funds caused him to move his temple to Guyana, South America, in 1977. The Jonestown settlement was to be a utopian commune, isolated from other populated areas.[60] At first, utopia was realized. Harmony thrived in the three hundred acres claimed from the tropical rain forest. A tidy life was built, a village grew, crops were grown, animals tended, children and the elderly cared for.[61] Membership in the commune included the relinquishing of personal assets to Jones, valued in the millions at the time. Membership appeared to be lifetime, as Jones asserted his leadership with beatings and threats of death. The power of "outside forces" were constantly assailed, and the solution of mass suicide was a repeated area of instruction.[62]

In the United States, the strident concerns of the families of the cult members resulted in the visit of Congressman Leo Ryan to the Jonestown commune to investigate. As he was about to leave four days later, with members of the commune who had chosen to defect, he and three newsmen were shot and killed. Fearing the reprisal of authorities, Jones enacted the scenario that his members had well rehearsed: mass suicide. Most apparently drank the cyanide punch without coercion. Some however, were forced to do so at gunpoint.

Hypodermic needles were used to spray the punch into the mouths of infants. The shot to the head that killed Jones was not, it was reported, inflicted by Jones himself. A total of 913 lives, including 276 children, were lost.[63]

In 1981, 22 year old Vernon Howell joined the Branch Davidians, a religious group headquartered outside of Waco, Texas. He had failed in his ambition to become a rock star. He began an affair with the self-proclaimed prophetess Lois Rodin, and following her death, struggled with her son George for leadership of the group. Driven off, Howell later returned with his followers and engaged in a gunfight with Rodin. In the legal proceedings that followed, a mistrial was declared. In 1990, Howell was the Branch Davidian leader. He took the name David Koresh, reflecting his declared assumption to the head of the House of David. Koresh is a derivation of the name Cyrus, the Persian King who freed the Jews held captive in Babylon.[64]

In 1993, Koresh declared "I am the lamb" and led his followers, stationed on their compound called "Ranch Apocalypse," in a stand off against Federal agents. Information had been leaked to agents regarding the arsenal of weapons stored on the Ranch. In reaction to a governmental assault roundly criticized for its incompetence, Koresh and his followers set the compound ablaze, immolating themselves.[65]

The April 7, 1997 cover of *Time*[66] displayed a startling picture of a man, taken from a video segment. It was a picture of Marshall Herff Applewhite, leader of the cult called Heaven's Gate. This image appeared to be designed to communicate the essence of this person's character. The man on the cover is uncomfortable for the viewer to regard, most notably for his eyes, which are unusually wide open, and threaten to overwhelm the observer with the force of their stare. His eye color, highlighted in tints of green, seems otherworldly. The knowledge that this man led 39 people to their deaths because of his vision, makes the image even more frightening.

Marshall Herff Applewhite was the son of a preacher, who gave up plans of the ministry in favor of a music career. He married, and with his wife and two children, struggled in a variety of jobs. By age 40, his apparent homosexuality was challenging his marriage, and the opportunity to take an operatic role came to naught. Homosexual affairs led to a stay at a psychiatric hospital, where Applewhite sought a "cure" for his sexual inclinations. Applewhite's response to his difficulties was the creation of a personal myth; he claimed he was becoming under the influence of "a being from the next level."[67] One of the nurses treating him, Bonnie Lu Nettles, developed a platonic relationship with him, and fed his burgeoning messianic fiction. By 1973, Applewhite and Nettles had concluded that they were the two witnesses prophesied by *Revelations* "to prepare the way to the kingdom of heaven."[68]

In their preaching, with the new musically assigned names of "Do" and "Ti," Applewhite and Nettles spoke with formidable passion of the need of followers "to renounce their families, sex, and drugs, and to pool their money with promises of a voyage to salvation on a spaceship." Their presentations played to packed houses.[69] Sadly for Applewhite, "Ti" Nettles died in 1985, just as their cult was receiving national attention.

Following Ti's death, the cult became increasingly absorbed in non-sexuality. Members started to wear baggy clothes and short hair to blur sexual identity. Applewhite, as well as five of his followers, were voluntarily castrated.[70]

The arrival of the Hale-Bopp comet was the apparent fulfillment of Applewhite's preachings. In the belief that a UFO was following the comet, Applewhite and his followers prepared to intercept the vehicle and attain their salvation. In an eerily organized fashion, the 39 members of the Heaven's Gate cult, in their neatly maintained rented mansion in Rancho Mirage, consumed phenobarbital and vodka, placed plastic bags over their heads, and lay in bed covered by purple shrouds. They slipped into unconsciousness, and finally death, anticipating their cosmic encounter.

The coverage in *Time* included the observation that the Heaven's Gate mass suicide was the fulfillment of predictions of catastrophe coinciding with the coming millennium, noting "the rise in the number of obscure cults and the increasingly fevered pitch of their rantings."[71]

Above Jim Jones' throne in the Jonestown commune were the words of George Santayana, "Those who do not remember the past are doomed to repeat it." The meaning of this quote to Jones and his followers is unknown. Its warning or prophecy to the needy in an apocalyptic time, however, is worth heeding.[72]

Chapter Six Bibliography

1. Nuhrah, A., (p. 521). In: Ebel, H. et. al. (1978). "A Close Encounter With the Millennium." *Journal of Psychohistory,* 5 (4), 499-522.

2. Boice, R., et. al. (1977). "Fin de Siecle." *American Psychologist,* 32 (12), 1121-1122.

3. *Ibid.,* (p. 1121).

4. *Ibid.*

5. Bisland, E. (1901). "The Time Spirit of the Twentieth Century." *Atlantic Monthly,* 87, 15-22. In: Boice, R., et. al. (1977). "Fin de Siecle." American Psychologist, 32(12), 1121-1122.

6. *Ibid.,* (p. 1122).

7. Axelrod, A., and Phillips, C. (1995). *What Everyone Should Know About the Twentieth Century.* (p.1-2). Holbrook: Adams Media Corporation.

8. *Ibid.,* (p. 5).

9. *Ibid.,* (p. 9-10).

10. *Ibid.,* (p. 33).

11. *Ibid.,* (p. 35).

12. *Ibid.,* (p. 174-175).

13. Lifton, R. J., (1993). *The Protean Self: Human Resilience in a Fragmented Age.* New York:Basic Books.

14. *Ibid.,* (p. 19).

15. *Ibid.*

16. *Ibid.,* (p. 21).

17. *Ibid.*

18. Ansbacher, H., and Ansbacher, R., (Eds.). (1956). *The Individual Psychology of Alfred Adler: a Systematic Presentation in Selections of his Writings.* (p. 277). New York: Harper Torchbooks.

19. *Ibid.*

20. *Ibid.*

21. Lifton, R. J., and Markusen, E., (1990). *The Genocidal Mentality.* (p. 10). New York: Basic Books.

22. Gearhart, J. (1984). "The Counselor in the Nuclear World: a

Rationale for Awareness and Action." *Journal of Counseling and Development,* 63, 67-75.

23. *Ibid.*

24. Lifton, J. (1982). In Gearhart, J. (1984). "The Counselor in the Nuclear world: a Rationale for Awareness and Action." *Journal of Counseling and Development,* 63, 67-75.

25. Axelrod, A., and Phillips, C. (1995). *What Everyone Should Know About the Twentieth Century.* (p. 304). Holbrook: Adams Media Corporation.

26. *Ibid.*

27. Wills, J., and Storey, G., (1996). "Sea Empress' Spill is Bigger than 'Exxon Valdez.'" *The Shetland News.*

28. Axelrod, A., and Phillips, C. (1995). *What Everyone Should Know About the Twentieth Century.* (p. 297). Holbrook: Adams Media Corporation.

29. *Ibid.,* (p. 297-298).

30. Nando.net (1996). "Officials say Ebola Virus Strain that Killed Monkeys Poses no Threat to Humans." *San Antonio Express News.*

31. McGreal, S. (1996). Re: ebola in usa. *ippl@awod.com.*

32. Johnson, E., et. al. (1995). "Lethal Experimental Infections of Rhesus Monkeys by Aerosolized Ebola Virus." *International Journal of Experimental Pathology,* 76, 227-236.

33. Preston, R. (1994). *The Hot Zone.* New York: Doubleday.

34. Freud, S. (1921). Group Psychology and the Analysis of the Ego. (p. 68). New York: Bantam Books. In: Becker, E. (1973). *The Denial of Death.* (p. 133). New York: Free Press Paperbacks.

35. Becker, E. (1973). *The Denial of Death.* (p. 133). New York: Free Press Paperbacks.

36. Dowling, J. (1977). "Millennialism and Psychology." (p. 125). *Journal of Psychiatry,* 5 (1), 121-129.

37. Saliba, J. (1995). *Understanding New Religious Movements.* (p. 75). Grand Rapids: Eerdmans Publishing Company.

38. Ibid., (p. 7).

39. Motivation. (1996). *Microsoft Encarta Encyclopedia.*

40. Saliba, J. (1995). *Understanding New Religious Movements.* (p. 1). Grand Rapids: Eerdmans Publishing Company.

41. *Ibid.,* (p. 6).

42. *Ibid.,* (p. 5).

43. *Ibid.*

44. Morse. F. (1980). *The Shakers and the World's People.* (p. xv). Hanover: University Press of New England.

45. *Ibid.,* (p. xvi).

46. *Ibid.,* (p. 10).

47. Moss-Kanter, R. (1972). "Commitment and the Internal Organization of Millennial Movements." *American Behavioral Scientist,* 16 (2), 219-243.

48. *Ibid.,* (p. 222).

49. *Ibid.,* (p. 224).

50. *Ibid.,* (p. 224-225).

51. *Ibid.,* (p. 227-228).

52. *Ibid.,* (p. 229).

53. *Ibid.,* (p. 231).

54. *Ibid.,* (p. 234).

55. *Ibid.,* (p. 233).

56. *Ibid.,* (p. 238).

57. Messiah. (1996). *Microsoft Encarta Encyclopedia.*

58. Kroth, J. (1984). "Recapitulating Jonestown." *The Journal Of Psychohistory,* 11 (3), Winter 1984, 383-393.

59. *Ibid.,* (p. 384).

60. Axelrod, A., and Phillips, C. (1995). *What Everyone Should Know About the Twentieth Century.* (p. 280). Holbrook: Adams Media Corporation.

61. *Associated Press,* (1997). "Jonestown Suicides Shocked World."

62. Axelrod, A., and Phillips, C. (1995). *What Everyone Should Know About the Twentieth Century.* (p. 280). Holbrook: Adams Media Corporation.

63. *Ibid.*

64. Frontline/WGBH Educational Foundation/*www.wgbh.org.* Biography:David Koresh.

65. Axelrod, A., and Phillips, C. (1995). *What Everyone Should Know About the Twentieth Century.* (p. 280). Holbrook: Adams Media Corporation.

66. *Time,* 149 (14). April 7, 1997.

67. Chua-Eoan, H. (1997). "Imprisoned by His Own Passions." *Time,* 149 (14), 40-42.

68. *Ibid.*

69. *Ibid.*

70. *Ibid.*

71. Gleick, E. (1997). "The Marker We've Been Waiting for." *Time,* 149 (14), 28-36.

72. Kroth, J. (1984). "Recapitulating Jonestown." *The Journal Of Psychohistory,* 11 (3), Winter 1984, 383-393.

Chapter Seven

Prophecy

"But do not trust any and every spirit, my friends; test the spirits, to see whether they are from God, for there are many prophets falsely inspired."1

THE NEED FOR PROPHECY

Prophecy has an aura. A gift given to a select few to see into the future, it is usually regarded as the product of some divine intervention. That aspect will be discussed, but seeing the future can first be explained as a more mundane, simple need that aids in our existence. This is probably best characterized by the less loaded term called *prediction*. Prediction is the process of utilizing information already known, *experience*, to make a statement of events that are to come. Our earliest ancestors used their experience with the weather, for example, to predict the outcome of the crops they had planted. Since their very existence depended on the harvest, farmers needed to make plans accordingly.

In our contemporary world, prediction is commonplace. The advance of science and mathematics, aided by the phenomenon of the computer, has turned prediction into an industry. Weather forecasting, economic trends, and investment projection are relied upon in our daily lives. Clearly, the ability to predict floods, hurricanes, and other natural disasters has saved many lives, enabling potential victims to be evacuated before a natural onslaught. Even in the world of sports and entertainment, prediction is relied upon to assist enthusiasts in the pursuit called gambling.2

The gift, or curse, of the intelligence of man is the painful awareness that his existence must conclude, for his observations of nature have well instructed him that all things have a beginning and an end. His ongoing concern over his history can be confined to a single question: *When?* In the pursuit of the answer to this simple but elusive question, prophecy finds its birth.

Sean M. O'Shea and Meryl A. Walker

The larger questions of existence, queries not answerable by simple prediction, provide the special aura that prophecy enjoys. The natural parameters of prediction are insufficient; the supernatural is required. Throughout history, those claiming to be prophetic have often been assigned the special status deemed appropriate for those who have a link with otherworldly powers. These special individuals have, through the experience called rapture, seen events elusive to the rest of their communities.

Detail from Sistine Chapel, *The Last Judgment,* Michaelangelo.

Prophecy, however, has an inherent problem. It is often not simply expressed. In our modern age, we are accustomed to, or even dependent upon, our local forecaster pronouncing, "tomorrow, it will rain." Following this prediction, we get up the next day and put on our raincoats, grab our umbrellas, and set off to work. Prophecy is not so simple. As the product of visions or dreams, prophecy is often expressed in *symbols*. Symbols, by their very nature, are subject to interpretation. More nebulously, the receipt of symbols by the purported prophet are *personal*, meaning that they are relevant to his/her experience. Any misinterpretation of the prophetic symbols, or misunderstanding of the personal experience of the prophet, renders the prophecy worthless. John of Patmos, in his *Revelations*, may serve as an example. John wrote in a time of extreme political persecution of his cult, Christianity. His vision, therefore, had to be expressed in terms that would not raise the ire of Rome. Thus, he employed an elaborate symbolism in his text, understandable to his followers, but only partially understood by later scholars. The same methodology can be applied to Nostradamus, who needed to avoid the wrath that one or another of his prophecies might cause. The seemingly endless number of books on the interpretation of visions, demonstrates our continuing need to see what the future holds.

There are, however, records of literal prophecies. An example, of course, is William Miller, who, as we have seen, boldly predicted that the world would end in 1843. Regardless of his adjustments to the timetable, it simply did not happen, leading to The Great Disappointment.

The need for prophecy can perhaps be seen more contemporarily in the reported rise in messianic movements, as well as in the tremendous success of "psychic hotlines." A call to a 1-900 number can provide, so the advertisements say, an interview with a "psychic," who will provide the caller with prophetic information about their personal future. The affiliation of well-known celebrities only adds to their allure.

MILLENNIAL PREDICTIONS

Accounts of prophecy are legion, and there will be no attempt made here to duplicate what many books have already exhaustively reported. A few examples, however, are mentionable because of their interest.

The Maya civilization is a celebrated one, renowned for its astronomy, organization, and sophistication, which was equal to the Aztecs. The Mayas were a group of Native Meso-American city-states that flourished in Mexico, originating in the Yucatan peninsula and further east. Their origins are unknown, but records point to a history dating as far back as 1500 B.C.E. The Maya Classical period, dating from 200-900 C.E., saw the establishment of great cultural centers.[3]

These centers are the reason that the Maya have received their acclaim. Their exceptional architecture included pyramids complexes capped by temples built around large plazas. The splendor of their ruins continue to be enjoyed by many tourists. Typical of an advanced ancient civilization, the Maya have left us some recorded history, having mastered writing in hieroglyphic form. Their interests in agriculture, weather, disease, hunting, and astronomy survive in codices housed in Dresden, Paris, and Madrid.[4] Maya descendants still inhabit Mexico, and part of what they maintain of their culture includes the Maya timekeeping system. The Maya had established an elaborate calendar structure, consisting of three simultaneous calendars, that was the most accurate known[5] prior to the establishment of the Gregorian calendar in 1592. Studies of the details of the Maya calendar describe movements through cycles lasting 20 years, 400 years, and 8000 years. Some students of the Maya calendar have determined that the completion of combinations of these three cycles will correspond with the conclusion of a more formidable Maya cycle of 160,000 years on, to be exact, December 22, 2012. The approach of this date will be marked by the "collapse of linear time-based conceptual structures."[6]

The accuracy of prophets has rightly been seen as an evaluation of their legitimacy. Even allowing for the variability in symbolic interpretation, Malachy O'Morgair is an interesting prophet. While not a millennial prophet in the strict sense, since he did not foretell an Apocalypse with the turn of the millennium, he did predict an end that is simply not too far away. Malachy was a follower of Saint Patrick, and had a successful, if somewhat difficult, career in the Irish church in the twelfth century. His good works and reported miracles were rewarded, however, when he was canonized in 1199.[7] Upon his death in 1184, he left behind a series of phrases that described the identity of all the popes that were to serve the church, right through the twentieth century, *800 years later.*[8] While substantial liberty has to be applied to the interpretations of Malachy's labels, they are interesting nonetheless.

Of contemporary Popes, John XXIII was labeled by Malachy *Pastor et Nauta*, Pastor of the Sea, interpreted by observers as a reference to John's tenure as Patriarch of Venice. Paul VI was assigned the designation *Flors Florum*, Flower of Flowers, a label perceived as referring to the fleurs-de-lys in his coat of arms. John-Paul I, a Pope who served for only thirty-three days, was given *De Medietate Lunae*, Of the Half Moon, which could refer to his demise in the middle of the month. John-Paul II, our present Pope, was stamped by Malachy as *De Labore Solis,* Labor of the Sun. Part of John-Paul's history included labor in a camp while a Polish prelate. Following the present Pope, Malachy lists only two additional popes. The successor to John-Paul II has been labeled by Malachy as *Gloriae Olivae.* Following him is *Petrus Romanus, Peter of Rome,* the last Pope, who is interpreted as the presage to the Last Judgement.[9]

Certainly the most famous of prophets is Michel de Notredame. He is best known by the Latinized version of his name, Nostradamus. Nostradamus was a physician of note in sixteenth century France, having distinguished himself in the treatment of plague victims. The recognition of his medical expertise would later result in his appointment as court physician to Charles IX.[10] His personal life, however, was not without tragedy. His two children died at an early age, with his wife losing her life only a few years later.[11]

The sixteenth century European world of Nostradamus was one of great change, some of which we have already mentioned. In reaction to these events, which are said to have had substantial impact on him,[12] Nostradamus began to compose prophecies for his own interest, with their actual publication occurring much later. Public reception of his prophecies produced acclaim for his apparent gift from some, but derision from others.[13] Among Nostradamus' assertions was his calculation of the date of creation. Using the information available in *Genesis*, which includes the lengths of the characters' lives, among other descriptions of time, Nostradamus assigned a date to the creation of the world. At the time of his sixteenth century calculation, he indicated that the time period between the creation and the flood was 2106 years. He further determined that he was living 4173 years and eight months after the creation, placing it in the third millennium B.C.E.[14]

Nostradamus' fame comes from the publication of his predictions *Centuries* in 1555. The interpretation of his work has been an ongoing pastime for his many readers over the last 400 years. In fact Cheetam, one of Nostradamus' biographers, states that "Nostradamus is probably the only author who could claim that his work has never been out of print for over four hundred years, apart from the Bible."[14]

Nostradamus wrote his prophecies in *quatrains*, which are four line rhyming verses. What provides for the difficulty in their interpretation is the fact that their original composition was in "an enigmatic combination of French (in Provincial dialect), Latin, Greek, and Italian."[15] In addition, they are not written chronologically. These apparent efforts at confusion were self serving, protecting Nostradamus from any adverse reactions that his prophecies may have generated.[16] The symbolism used by Nostradamus also poses a challenge for the interpreter. While Nostradamus may have had a gift for predicting events far into the future, he only had sixteenth century terminology at his disposal. How could a man of his era express "airplane," or "nuclear weapon?" Students of his work say that he was forced to use his available symbols, such as "flying insect," or "raging fire."[17]

One of the more notable quatrains actually uses the year 1999. It is shown here not only for its interest, but for the interpretative problems that typically confront the reader of Nostradamus.

> *The year 1999 and seventh month*
> *From the sky will come a great king of terror,*
> *To raise again the great king of Jacquerie*
> *Before and after, Mars will reign at will.*

Jacquerie is a term reported to refer to a bloody peasant revolt against the nobility in the fourteenth century.[18] The use of a celestial body, Mars, in a quatrain, is not unusual. Mars was the Roman god of war, so this could be a reference to widespread violence. A second interpretation relies on accepting that Nostradamus was deemed, in addition to his mastery of medicine and mathematics, to have been expert in astrology. One researcher, Timms, has suggested that this quatrain may refer to the known instability of the orbit of the Martian moon, Phobos. It has been hypothesized that this moon could possibly leave its Martian orbit and disastrously affect the earth.[19]

There is some discussion about just when the world is scheduled to end, according to Nostradamus. *Centuries* depicts the year 3797. Interpreters of his work, however, indicate that many of his darkest visions are confined to the time around 2000.[20] Nostradamus died on July 2, 1566, just as he had predicted.[21]

A more contemporary revelation of prophecy bears mention because of its unique and fascinating premise. Published just recently, *The Bible Code* documents the unlikely integration of the Bible with computer technology to produce prophecy.[22] The *Bible Code*, the author asserts, is the twentieth centruy breaking of the Biblical Seal. This work was written by Michael Drosnin, whose reporting credentials include work at *The Washington Post* and *The Wall Street Journal,* and who claims to be not religious.

The Bible Code was found to exist in the Hebrew version of the Old Testament. A rabbi and scholar in Czechoslovakia named Weissmandel discovered over fifty years ago that by skipping fifty letters, and then another fifty, and so on, the word Torah was spelled out in the Books of Genesis, Exodus, Numbers and Deuteronomy.[23] A code contained in the Bible had been suspected by Sir Isaac Newton as far back as the seventeenth century. Despite his reported obsession with finding the code, as reported by John Maynard Keynes, he failed.[24]

The application of computer technology, Drosnin reports, cracked the code, and statistics indicated that random chance was not at work. Findings stated the significance at *99.998%.* An expert in code at the National Security Agency, a skeptic, could not dispute the findings. The conclusion: "The Bible was encoded with information about the past and the future in a way that was mathematically beyond random chance, and was found in no other text."[25]

The Bible Code produced much more than the word *Torah.* In September 1994, Drosnin went to Israel to inform a friend of Prime Minister Yitzak Rabin that the Bible Code foretold the assassination of the prime minister. Fourteen months later, it happened. It seems that the assassination of Anwar Sadat, as well as the Kennedy brothers, was also foretold.[26]

The way that the code works is not easy to explain. In much the same way that the discovering rabbi tried, variable numbers of letters are skipped, and then one is selected, and so on. The selected letters form words that are the code. Simple skipping, however, makes the procedure seem less complex than it really is. Criss-crossing of text is also involved, hence the need for the computer to crack the code, break the Seal.[27]

The Bible Code makes other notable, and troubling predictions. The Hebrew year 5756, corresponding with 1995-1996, is labeled the beginning of the "End of Days." According to the Bible Code, the Apocalypse has already begun. It additionally foretells "Atomic Holocaust" in the years 2000-2006. Its perpetrator? The Bible Code tells us, "Syria."[28] In conclusion, Drosnin tells us that the Bible Code predicts a future of multiple scenarios, some of which can be averted. Ultimately, it seems we are the authors of our own destiny.

WHEN A PROPHETIC DREAM DIES

Regardless of differences in religious, philosophical, or ideological approaches, millennarian movements share one important trait. The current social order is slated for dramatic change in the realizable future, as the product of some transcendent occurrence.[29] The expectation of this occurrence is usually recorded through a seer or prophet's vision, which has come to that individual through the experience of rapture. The articulation of the vision, which is the description of events yet to come, draws those who seek to benefit from that prophecy.

Prospective prophets have two options in the expression of their visions. One, the more difficult, is to provide some realm of exactitude to the appearance of the anticipated event. Evidently, this has been shown to be an approach that is less wise, given the historical precedents for prophetic failure. The Millerites, as we have said, experienced a Great Disappointment, when the heralded millennium of William Miller did not arrive as expected in 1843 or 1844. Prophecy is more commonly ambiguous, as we have just discussed. This ambiguity in the prophetic vision of John of Patmos, *Revelations*, has given it a life that approaches 2,000 years.

Although still unfulfilled, the millennium myth continues to be anticipated because each succeeding generation can apply the nebulous and universal images to their own reality and to their own needs.

The danger posed to the longevity of millennarian movements are the factors implicit in the dynamics of any group. "Emotional contagion and rumor creation"[30] are both familiar to us from our workplace. The rumor of a change in the hierarchy of our work organization, or even in the peccadilloes of our co-workers, quickly spreads, only to die in the presence of an additional rumor that captivates our attention anew. Sustenance, in short, is required for maintenance.[31]

The sustenance of a millennarian group can be accomplished in a variety of ways. Borrowing from established mainstream groups, millennarian groups can provide stable leadership, as well as an ideology that is more broad than narrow; essentially, a redefinition of the focus of their birth.[32] "Ideological rationalization, explanation, reinterpretation, or denial" can also be employed as measures to ensure that the millennial hope will endure.[33] Finally, absolute withdrawal, as we have seen with Jonestown and the Shakers, is also an option.

The anticipated arrival of a millennial event requires significant preparation. The media occasionally depict the industrious activity that absorbs groups as well as individuals who are awaiting a cataclysm. The participants are seen storing food, water, and weapons to ensure their survival when the *event* occurs.[34] *Just in case;* one media report highlighted a company that manufactured prefabricated "domiciles" to be buried in customers' backyards. The residence would store substantial foodstuffs, as well as accommodate the breathing and toiletry needs of its occupants. The settlements of doomsday subscribers have found homes in the less populated states of the west. In their pursuit, they share state residency with militia groups, who have their own vision of a millennium. The militia vision may be seen as their correction of the corruption perceived to exist in "government, the media, and the secret powers that govern our planet."[35]

A converse reaction to the impending millennium is consumption. With an impending delivery awaiting, participants in a millennial movement might decide, in a moment of jubilation, to consume lasciviously, which would deplete or even destroy resources.[36]

The ultimate shock to a prophetic movement is the non-fulfillment of the guiding prophecy. Entire lives have been reorganized, commitments made, endless labors executed, all for nothing. Shock and

surprise, disappointment and dismay, bewilderment and disorienta-
tion all reign, whether exclusively or in combination. Disengagement
from the movement may be sought, or the rise of a new leadership
with a new vision may result. The entire disintegration of the group
is also an obvious possibility.[37]

The integrity of a movement can, however, be maintained in the
face of prophetic failure, through the use of the simple assignment
of *blame*. This assertion can take a variety of forms. A misinterpretation of signs can be suggested. The influence of evil can be cited.
Or ultimately, the blame can be assigned to the followers of the
movement themselves. The commitment of the followers may be
deemed suspect in its intensity, or any other indication that points
to "unreadiness."[38] An example is that of the Church Universal and
Triumphant, based in Montana. Elizabeth Clare Prophet, the head of
the church, declared that nuclear war would occur on April 23, 1990.
In response, several thousand of her adherents made appropriate
arrangements by seeking the safety of fallout shelters.[39] In the wake
of this inaccuracy, her church still thrives. What may be derived in
the face of prophetic failure is the notion that *we didn't get it right.*
Failure is not unknown to many movement adherents, and so, as we
saw in both Colonial and Civil War America, a renewed proselytizing
is perceived to be the answer. And in this renewal, a movement lives
on.

Finally, in the way of commentary, there remains a final variety of
prophecy that can be extremely potent in a society. That prophecy
is *self-fulfilling prophecy.* Any society that is preoccupied with doom
will live in an existence that precludes any other scenario. In that
very preoccupation, other issues and concerns that might contribute to such an outcome will be neglected. And in that insensitiv-
ity, disregard, and procrastination, we will surely find our
Apocalypse.

Chapter Seven Bibliography

1. Kay, T. (1997). *When the Comet Runs.* (p. 16). Charlottesville: Hampton Roads Publishing.
2. Mann, AT (1992). *Millennium Prophecies.* (p. 3). Reexport: Element Books.
3. Rosenberg, M. (1996). Maya. *Microsoft Encarta Encyclopedia.*
4. *Ibid.*
5. *Ibid.*
6. Rice, M. and Jeada, Y. (1997). Introduction to the Mayan Calendar. *www.resonate.com.*
7. Malachy, Saint. (1996). *Microsoft Encart Encyclopedia.*
8. Mann, AT (1992). *Millennium Prophecies.* (p. 79). Reexport: Element Books.
9. *Ibid.,* (p. 80).
10. Kay, T. (1997). *When the Comet Runs.* (p. 16). Charlottesville: Hampton Roads Publishing.
11. Mann, AT (1992). *Millennium Prophecies.* (p. 52). Reexport: Element Books.
12. *Ibid.*
13. *Ibid.*
14. Cheetham, E. (1981). *The Man who Saw Tomorrow.* New York: Berkley Books.
15. Mann, AT (1992). *Millennium Prophecies.* (p. 52). Reexport: Element Books.
16. *Ibid.*
17. *Ibid.,* (p. 54).
18. Kay, T. (1997). *When the Comet Runs.* (p. 40). Charlottesville: Hampton Roads Publishing.
19. *Ibid.*
20. Mann, AT (1992). *Millennium Prophecies.* (p. 58). Reexport: Element Books.
21. *Ibid.,* (p. 53).
22. Drosnin, M. (1997). *The Bible Code.* New York: Simon and Schuster.
23. *Ibid.,* (p. 20).

24. *Ibid.,* (p. 21).

25. *Ibid.,* (p. 23-24).

26. *Ibid.,* (p. 13).

27. *Ibid.,* (p. 25).

28. *Ibid.,* (p. 134).

29. Cohn, N.(1962). In: Zygmunt, J. (1972). "When Prophecies Fail: a Theoretical Perspective on the Comparative Evidence." *American Behavioral Scientist,* 16(2), 245-268.

30. Zygmunt, J. (1972). "When Prophecies Fail: a Theoretical Perspective on the Comparative Evidence." *American Behavioral Scientist,* 16 (2), 245-268.

31. *Ibid.,* (p. 249).

32. *Ibid.,* (p. 250).

33. *Ibid.*

34. *Ibid.,* (p. 254).

35. Vogel, J. (1997). Extreme web. *editor@village voice.com.*

36. Zygmunt, J. (1972). "When Prophecies Fail: a Theoretical Perspective on the Comparative Evidence." *American Behavorial Scientist,* 16 (2), 245-268.

37. *Ibid.,* (p. 258).

38. *Ibid.,* (p. 260-261).

39. *New York Times,* March 15, 1990.

Chapter Eight

The Millennium As Metaphor

"Millennium fever possesses popular
culture like a doomsday virus."1

APOCALYPTIC FANTASIES

In our exploration of millennial thought, we have touched upon the
roles of mythology, history, and religion, as well as the implicit
involvement of politics, prophecy, and charlatans. Perhaps at this
point, the clinical perspective merits our attention. The meaning of
Apocalypse, taken from its Greek roots, means "to reveal" or "to
uncover."2 The clinical evaluation of apocalyptic dreams and fantasies makes this definition particularly apt, because of what these
images disclose about those experiencing them.

The Apocalyptic scenario is familiar to us as the sense that the
extant world is due for destruction, with a subsequent existence,
whatever its form, to follow. The participation of an integral figure, a
messiah, is also part of the process.

Ostrow states that apocalyptic images are not at all unusual presentations in patients seen in psychiatric and psychoanalytic practice. Apocalyptic fantasies and dreams, Ostrow notes, are a form of
expression for the patient. This expression is concurrent with
episodes that need to accommodate a feeling of rage. The inner conflict that is experienced by the patient is "projected onto a cosmic
screen."3 This is apparently the reason that apocalyptic scenarios
have been widely portrayed as occurring on a stage that includes
the entire earth as well as the heavens above it. The rebirth of the
world commensurate with such visions, is, Ostrow continues, a rep-
resentation of reentry into the mother's body, or paradise. The fear-
some and gruesome beasts encountered in the process of this cosmic story are representatives of the father and/or siblings.4

Ostrow, despite extensive experience with this matter, "has not

The Last Judgment: Central Panel, Hieronymus Bosch.

been able to decide whether the psyche contains an archetype of the apocalypse."[5]

There has been much written about dreams, and clinicians have paid much attention to their import. An established assessment of dreams finds them to be an individual's avenue for the solving of problems, as well as for finding guidance for the future. Dreams are, Adler says, "the bridge that connects the problem which confronts the dreamer, with the goal of his attainment... it shows his opinion of his own nature and of the nature and meaning of life."[6]

Dreams are scripted in symbols, and the interpretation of those symbols tell us much about the motivations of the dreamer. Apocalyptic dreams have their own symbolic language. One symbol is that of the *moving vehicle*, which, regardless of presentation, is understood to represent escape from the scene of destruction, which is the dreamer's rage.[7] This recalls the preoccupation of Applewhite and the Heaven's Gate cult with a UFO encounter. Another symbol is *color, light, and shimmering luminescence*. This symbol depicts an urgent desire for merging with a Deity. While god-figures are typically male fatherly renderings, the actuality here is for union with the mother.[8]

Falling objects represent destruction.[9] A common theme in End of Days scenarios are, as we have seen, "things coming down from the heavens." Whether fire and brimstone, celestial bodies, or nuclear missiles, a catastrophic outcome follows. *Rising objects* depict the opposite. This symbol implies safety, protection, and the messian-ic.[10] A reference to a movie illustrates this wonderfully. At the conclusion of the film *Close Encounters of the Third Kind*, the lead character of the film, Roy Neary, prepares to board the awesome spaceship. Surrounded by otherworldly beings, he enters the craft. He has been *chosen*. The craft majestically takes off, headed to another world.[11]

With the awareness of the *Book of Revelations* being the prominent Apocalypse in the Christian world, we move to the next symbol which is *revelation of a secret*.[12] This symbol points to the solutions to problems, seen here as the patient's issues with rage, that will somehow be solved through a magical answer, one that only needs to be unencrypted. In this symbol, knowledge truly is power, because once armed with the might of this enchanted secret, the dreamer transforms into a messiah.

Angels are frequent players on the apocalyptic stage. Over recent years, they have enjoyed a notable renaissance in popular culture.

Books, movies, and television programs show the roles that angels have played in the daily lives of their adherents. Symbolically, in apocalyptic dreams angels are often depicted as being "robed in linen," and represent a parent figure. On occasion, angels can be portrayed as hostile beings;[13] after all, Satan is a fallen angel.

The clinical understanding of apocalyptic thinking is important, because it is an integral part of the vision that guides religious movements and governments alike.[14] The basis of such thinking, found in rage, demands our attention. Ostrow reminds us that mood "tends to become generalized and uniform within the social group, and to find appropriate media for expression."[15] The anxieties and tension so prevalent in contemporary life impact all of us, imbuing a corresponding apocalyptic aura. Implied in this is some kind of social response, based in desperation, longing for the salvation of hope and inspiration. The millennial visions that will be created in the perception of need, regardless of their apparent folly, will surely find adherents.

THE MILLENNIUM IN POPULAR CULTURE

We can see our reflection in the media that envelopes us. Our popular culture represents, in print and image, who we are, what we desire and abhor, and what intrigues us. A casual perusal of recent movie listings or a television guide or a stroll through a bookstore can serve as an informal barometer of societal interest. Ranking high in any inventory of topics appealing to our culture is the *paranormal*. For our purposes, paranormal generically refers to phenomena whose existence is inconsistent with the familiar properties of day-to-day experience. Examples of parapsychological events might include miracles, out-of-body experiences, UFOs, encounters with angels, or events surrounding the presence of alien beings. Multiple other examples could be provided. Since the media is a business whose monetary success is commensurate with their ability to provide what we want, they have provided us with paranormal entertainment in copious quantities.

Movies such as *The Star Wars Trilogy, Close Encounters of the Third Kind, E.T., Independence Day,* and *Men in Black* all deal with alien interactions of distinctly different types, and are among the most profitable movies ever made. Television programs have followed suit. *The X-Files* routinely deals with paranormal phenomena such as

UFOs, as well as with individuals who possess extraordinary powers. The four versions of *Star Trek* highlight technological advances and occasionally problematic co-existence with a vast array of alien life forms. Even educationally oriented programs, such as on The Learning Channel, produce programs such as *Mysteries of the Millennium*, about predictions of our demise.

The medium of print overflows with books about the paranormal, with many recent bestsellers regarding out-of-body experiences. There are many books available that inform us about ghosts, witchcraft, psychics, and now the millennium. And in addition to the realm of book publishing, news magazines such as *Time* and *Newsweek* have, during the past year, featured issues with cover stories about the appetite for the paranormal.

The advances of special effects technology in films have produced characters, locations, vehicles, powers, and catastrophic effects that could only be imagined in the past. Science fiction, as Ebel says, becomes theology as modern myths are visualized. The power of the film *Star Wars* was in the appeal made to viewers with the affirmation to believe in "the Force."[16] Depicted in *Star Wars,* psychologists say, are images that describe the emotional character of a people living in an era fraught with signs of demise. Darth Vader, for example, is the image of the need of our culture for "a diabolical projective embodiment of aggressions we cannot yet therapeutically confront and internalize."[17] He also, sadly, represents the absence of humanity in the world. His mask tells us that he is no longer a person, but forced to live under the terms of a system imposed upon him. We can identify with him because we may also, in our daily lives, feel under the imposition of some system dominating our existence.[18]

A related symbol is that of the Death Star, the enormous planet-sized vessel of destruction that is home to Darth Vader and the evil forces of the Galactic Empire. This "social machine" is maintained by the labors of droves of masked inhabitants. They conduct their business as apparent automatons, additional components in the machinery of their world.[19] This reflects feelings we may have about our own planet, where industry rules, and our vigilant maintenance of machinery is demanded. *Star Wars* embodies an ardent wish that somehow, like Luke Skywalker and Han Solo, we will be capable, through the remnants of our more noble qualities, of banding together and destroying the Death Star aspects of our planet.[20]

Close Encounters of the Third Kind is a film that expresses another group desire, the promise of rebirth. Briefly it recounts the events in the life of Roy Neary, an unexceptional person, like most of us, previous to his encounter with a UFO. Following his extraordinary experience, Roy has visions of a mountain, visions that become an obsession, eventually costing him his family. Roy sees a story about the mountain on a television news cast, and immediately sets off on a quest to get there, along with a woman who has had a similar experience. At the site, a meeting between the UFO occupants and the government is planned. Victorious over multiple challenges to keep him from the site, he is present for the rendezvous. Discovering that his experience had determined him to be chosen, he boards the UFO, leaving this world.[21]

The response to this film was tremendous, and its spectacular ending was part of a religious aura that enveloped the production. The encounter with the UFO is a religious event for Roy, one that sends him on a mission to seek the truth, despite the substantial cost of his family, his job, and his friends. He rejects all of the trappings of middle-class life and perseveres in his mission. In the end, his efforts and his faith are rewarded with an encounter with a supreme being, represented on the screen by an enormous and magnificently colored UFO.[22]

The film has millennial overtones as well. Roy's encounter with the UFO depicts the wonder and splendor that supposedly awaits us in the Second Coming. Other millennial themes, such as dissatisfaction with the nature of our current existence and rebirth into a new and better world, are also illustrated.[23]

The 1996 film *Independence Day*, essentially a comic book for the screen, presented another meeting of man and alien. Our visitors make quite a dramatic entrance, arriving in flying saucers so large that sunlight is blocked as they pass overhead, entering every major city in the world. These beings are not to be confused with the spiritual visitors of *Close Encounters*. They coldly proceed to deliver destruction from the heavens, destroying all world capitals. The film illustrates how the virtues of cooperation and sacrifice, combined with the guidance of a warrior-leader, prevail over evil in an Apocalypse scenario.

This film was bluntly millennial, with abundant scenes of elabo-

Detail from Sistine Chapel, *The Last Judgment,* Michaelangelo.

rate destruction raining down from the heavens, a seemingly endless plague of alien-insect creatures, and our sense of weakness related to our survival at the hands of other forces. Interestingly, the film alludes to government agencies that have covered up their possession of alien craft and corpses, knowledge kept even from the President. The relevance of this episode in the film to popular belief will be mentioned shortly. A co-producer of the movie stated that the theme of the movie was the question: "How will we react at the end of the world?"[24]

These films serve as illustrators of the continuing discussion regarding the existence of UFOs and aliens. A 1996 *Newsweek* poll found that in the United States, 48% of Americans believe that UFOs are real, and 29% think that alien contact has been made. Another 48% believe that there is a government conspiracy to cover up such matters.[25] Clearly, belief in these matters is not confined to a small group of people.

UFOs appear to have an extensive recorded history, dependant, of course, on the supportive perspective of the reader of the records. Alien and UFO encounters have been assigned to Ezekiel in the Old Testament, as well as the Emperor Constantine. Sixteenth century records describe the sighting of black discs in the sky, apparently in combat with one another. Late nineteenth century sightings include that of a "dirigible shaped craft" seen over a period of five months by thousands in the state of California.

An unusual encounter is reported to have occurred in Leroy, Kansas, on April 19, 1897. Alexander Hamilton, a farmer who earlier in his life was a United States congressman, was awakened by a commotion among his livestock. When he went out to investigate, he reported seeing a craft in the sky that was clearly in descent. He went to get his son and his farmhand. The trio observed a craft 300 feet long, hovering 30 feet off the ground. The ship was close enough to observe the six strange beings inside a transparent encasement beneath the craft. The beings shone a light on the observers, then proceeded to elevate the craft and leave, but not before capturing a calf, using an appendage of the craft. The craft then rose and left with the animal. On the following day, the remains of the animal were found.

World War II produced reports of pilots observing balls of light that sometimes seemed to pursue their airplanes.[26] Following the war, reports grew to be legion, familiar to many of us through substantial media accounts.

Clinical and theoretical speculations about the nature of UFOs are well documented by Byran in his book, *Close Encounters of the Fourth Kind: Alien Abduction, UFOs, and the Conference at M.I.T.* Included in this book is a presentation of Jung, who published his own impressions about the UFO phenomenon in 1959. Jung found UFOs to be a challenging subject with no easy answers. He speculated that the objects were "weightless thoughts," or "materialized psychisms," meaning apparent entities devised by the collective unconscious.[27] The historical and widespread appearance of UFOs seemed to be supportive of Jung's contention that there is a collective unconscious, from which there emerge images that are shared by all people.[28]

Jung goes on to say that the sightings also stem from *need*. The sight of food, he explains, satisfies our physical hunger, "so, the hunger of the soul is sated by the vision of numinous images," because of a lack of the "*actual and immediate experience of spiritual reality.*"[29] In fiery images there is an ambiguity, for it portents salvation and destruction at the same time. "What it will be, for good or ill depends on the understanding and ethical decision of the individual." It appears as a message to "modern man admonishing him to meditate on the signs in the heavens and to interpret them aright."[30]

"The logical result is a hunger for anything extraordinary. If we add to this the great defeat of human reason, daily demonstrated in the newspapers and rendered even more menacing by the incalculable dangers of the hydrogen bomb, the picture that unfolds before us is one of universal distress, comparable to the situation at the beginning of our era, or to the chaos that followed A. D. 1000..." Given our failures, and our distress, Jung concludes, a search of the heavens for a miracle is not at all surprising.[31]

A WISH FOR THE COMING MILLENNIUM

Our brief review of history, mythology, religion, and related topics has produced one inescapable notion; *existence is not guaranteed.* This troubling thought is doubly devious as it reflects our own struggles with the sense of our personal death, as well as with the end of the world. Somehow, whether in the outward practice of religion, or through the recognition of a voice within, or both, we contend as best we can with this reality. The ability to plan for the future that has allowed our species to survive goes on, although an awareness of current events sparks an occasional, if not frequent, glimmer of realization that these efforts may be in vain.

The millennium represents a transition, personal and societal, that has been anticipated since antiquity. There have been tremendous efforts expended to ascertain a date and a year for such a transformation, none of which have been accurate thus far. A societal cataclysm commensurate with a millennial disaster could occur at any time, as we are painfully aware, from sources that are numerous.

Personal transformation, too, can come at any time. There is no way to determine when, in the course of living through daily routine, something will cross your path, vision, or perception, and generate an awareness in you that will forever change who you are, how you think, and what you feel. Perhaps the millennium has already occurred, and you are now proceeding through life benevolently and gracefully transformed.

For many, such an occurrence awaits an assigned date, whether in 2000, or 2001. For those motivated to positively transform at that time, millennial hype will have been valuable. For the scoffers and skeptics of transformation, it will be back to business as usual, which society can ill afford.

The change of the millennium is truly an unusual event. Records from the millennium of 1000 are insufficient for a detailed grasp of its manifestations. But media reports already available indicate that the coming millenium may arrive in a cloud of jaded malaise, with planners seeking to celebrate as with any other New Year's Eve, save for unusual excess. The shift into the twenty-first century cannot be downplayed as a simple change of number. To minimize this event is to employ a prevalent and dangerous mechanism called *denial*. To deny the importance of the role of the millennium in our history and our religions is the denial of possibility, the denial of a belief that we can rescue ourselves from the threatening sense of loss of control in the present, which is a surviving legacy of the past.

We have learned that the millennium is loaded with the sadness of human yearning, the perceived decrepitude of society, and our need for an existence that equals the comfort we felt in the womb. We project onto the heavens an urgency to be cared for, as well as the nightmare of our destruction.

We close with our wish, however ideal, that the millennium comes to us as an anticipated gift. Once opened, its contents are cherished, its possibilities explored, and its very existence enhancing the promise of our own.

Chapter Eight Bibliography

1. Polito, R. (1996). "Apocalypse Now." *The New York Times Book Review,* October 20, 1996. (p.16).

2. Ostrow, M. (1986). "Archetypes of Apocalypse in Dreams and Fantasies, and in Religious Scripture." *American Imago,* 43 (4), 307- 334.

3. *Ibid.,* (p. 308)

4. *Ibid.*

5. *Ibid.,* (p. 309).

6. Ansbacher, H., and Ansbacher, R. (Eds.) (1956). *The Individual Psychology of Alfred Adler: a Systematic Presentation in Selections from his Writings.* (p. 359.) New York: Basic Books.

7. Ostrow, M. (1986). "Archetypes of Apocalypse in Dreams and Fantasies, and in Religious Scripture." *American Imago,* 43 (4), 307- 334.

8. *Ibid.,* (p. 314).

9. *Ibid.*

10. *Ibid.,* (p. 315).

11. Greco, M. et. al. (1978). "A Close Encounter with the Millennium." Journal of Psychohistory, 5 (4), 499-521.

12. Ostrow, M. (1986). "Archetypes of Apocalypse in Dreams and Fantasies, and in Religious Scripture." *American Imago,* 43 (4), 307- 334.

13. *Ibid.,* (p. 319).

14. *Ibid.,* (p. 326).

15. *Ibid.,* (p. 327).

16. Ebel, H. (1978). "The New Theology: Star Trek, Star Wars, Close Encounters, and the Crisis of Pseudo-rationality." *Journal of Psychohistory,* 5 (4), 487-497.

17. *Ibid.,* (p. 487).

18. Flowers, B. (Ed.). (1988). *Joseph Campbell: the Power of Myth with Bill Moyers.* (p. 144). New York: Doubleday.

19. Ebel, H. (1978). "The New Theology: Star Trek, Star Wars, Close Encounters, and the Crisis of Pseudo-rationality." *Journal of Psychohistory,* 5 (4), 487-497.

20. *Ibid.,* (p. 493).

21. Greco, M. et. al. (1978). "A Close Encounter with the Millennium." *Journal of Psychohistory,* 5 (4), 499-521.

22. *Ibid.*

23. *Ibid.*

24. Marin, R., (1996). "Alien Invasion!" *Newsweek,* July 8, 1996, 48-54.

25. *Ibid.*

26. Bryan, C. D. B., (1995). *Close Encounters of the Fourth Kind: Alien Abduction, UFOs, and the Conference at M.I.T.* (p. 426-428). New York: Alfred A. Knopf.

27. Jung, C. (1959). *Flying Saucers: a Modern Myth of Things Seen in the Sky.* New York: New American Library. In:Bryan, C. D. B., (1995). *Close Encounters of the Fourth Kind: Alien Abduction, UFOs, and the Conference at M.I.T.* (p. 434). New York: Alfred A. Knopf.

28. Bryan, C. D. B., (1995). *Close Encounters of the Fourth Kind: Alien Abduction, UFOs, and the Conference at M.I.T.* (p. 434). New York: Alfred A. Knopf.

29. Jung, C., (1978). *Flying Saucers.* (p. 36). New York: MJF Books.

30. *Ibid.,* (p. 83).

31. *Ibid.,* (p. 135).